This book brings together, in a no[...] academic way, a concise summary [...] research on spirituality/religion and health with a conservative Evangelical account of Christian faith. Not every Christian will agree with the theology, but I don't think that you have to agree with all that is said here in order to find this a helpful and thought-provoking book. The achievement of summarizing in one place an account of Christian faith and practice together with a summary of scientific findings on spirituality and health is rare.

—CHRIS COOK, BSC, MB, BS, MD, MA, PHD, FRCPSYCH
DEPARTMENT OF THEOLOGY AND RELIGION
DURHAM UNIVERSITY

For the serious religious reader this book will provide a review of the research on the interrelationships between religiousness and health. The kind of religiousness assumed is positive, from the heart, and devout, in contrast with those manifestations of religion that are hostile and violent—thus the book acknowledges that not all "religion" is the same. Within its intended orbit of discussion, the book draws parallels between various research findings and various religious, particularly Christian teachings. Questions and issues remain, of course. But at the root of the text is the fundamental principle that the processes involved in believing are what enable human wholeness to be what it is.

—RAYMOND F. PALOUTZIAN, PHD
COEDITOR, *HANDBOOK OF THE PSYCHOLOGY
OF RELIGION AND SPIRITUALITY*
AUTHOR, *INVITATION TO THE PSYCHOLOGY OF RELIGION*
EDITOR, *THE INTERNATIONAL JOURNAL FOR THE
PSYCHOLOGY OF RELIGION*

God is still in the business of healing. Intellectuals may dismiss this idea, and atheists may get upset that people believe in miracles. However, I am so grateful that my friend Max Fleury has challenged the status quo by reminding us that healing is real. Jesus Christ healed the sick, and He called His followers to do the same. The power of the Holy Spirit is still alive and well today, and followers of Christ must stretch their faith to expect God's supernatural power to work in their lives. If you need healing, this book will encourage you to believe in Christ's power. If you are a doubter, this book will challenge your opinions. Let's make room for the supernatural!

—J. Lee Grady
Former Editor, *Charisma Magazine*
Director, The Mordecai Project

The Faith Link is a most valuable contribution to the field of faith and health. The historical dimension of the relationship between faith and medicine offer a clarifying starting point, and sets up an outstanding presentation of the solid medical facts about healing, believing, and spirituality. This is an excellent book that clinicians, social workers, chaplains, and theologians can read with great benefit.

—Stephen G. Post, PhD
Professor of Preventive Medicine
Director, Center for Medical Humanities,
Compassionate Care, and Bioethics
Stony Brook University School of Medicine,
New York

There is a plethora of evidence that claims to connect religion with health. Max Fleury summarizes this in an open and accessible way, but does so with a particular angle. In a social and scientific context that favors universality over particularity, Fleury draws our attention to the fact that when we are talking about the relationship between religion and health, we are not simply talking about a general system of beliefs, we are talking about God; in this case the God that Christians have worshipped for thousands of years. Through an interesting blend of theology and science this book offers something that is missing from many similar texts: passion and commitment.

—JOHN SWINTON PhD, RMN, RNMD
PROFESSOR, PRACTICAL THEOLOGY AND PASTORAL CARE
DIRECTOR, CENTRE FOR SPIRITUALITY,
HEALTH AND DISABILITY
UNIVERSITY OF ABERDEEN
SCOTLAND
UNITED KINGDOM

THE
FAITH
LINK

MAX FLEURY, MD

CHARISMA
HOUSE

Most CHARISMA HOUSE BOOK GROUP products are available at special quantity discounts for bulk purchase for sales promotions, premiums, fund-raising, and educational needs. For details, write Charisma House Book Group, 600 Rinehart Road, Lake Mary, Florida 32746, or telephone (407) 333-0600.

THE FAITH LINK by Max Fleury, MD
Published by Charisma House
Charisma Media/Charisma House Book Group
600 Rinehart Road
Lake Mary, Florida 32746
www.charismahouse.com

Translation from the French: Mary Frances Knapp

Cover design by Vincent Pirozzi
Design Director: Justin Evans

Visit the author's website at www.maxfleury.com.

Library of Congress Cataloging-in-Publication Data:
An application to register this book for cataloging has been
submitted to the Library of Congress.

International Standard Book Number: 978-1-62998-630-2
E-book ISBN: 978-1-62998-631-9

First edition

16 17 18 19 20 — 987654321
Printed in the United States of America

To Valérie, my beloved wife, and Timothée, Evodie, Paul, and Noémi, my wonderful children, for their unconditional love and support.

To Eskil Ullberg, who opened me up to an unlimited sphere of action: that of faith.

CONTENTS

FOREWORD

THE PREMISE OF this book, which Dr. Fleury so clearly develops, is that gospel values—when applied to everyday life—seem to lead to a healthy, balanced, and fulfilled existence. Written for the Christian reader, this wonderful volume encourages people to place their confidence in God concerning their health and healing. It backs up this recommendation with a wide range of scientific studies.

Besides surveying the research, Dr. Fleury also discusses a wide range of topics related to Christian spirituality. These will be informative to the reader, whether an interested layperson, clergyperson, medical professional, or a theology professor. This information is provided in a readable format and engages the intellect and the spirit. Nowhere, however, does Dr. Fleury say that people with a medical illness should pursue faith alone or avoid medical care. When used together, these twin healing disciplines work marvelously. They don't function so well when used to the exclusion of the other.

As a scientist who conducts this type of research, trains others to do so, and carefully follows the studies emerging in this field, I can say confidently that published research continues to show a connection between deep religious faith and all aspects of good health, whether social, behavioral, mental, or physical.

For nearly thirty years I've been interested in the relationship between religious belief and commitment to almost every aspect of mental and physical health. In my training as a nurse, a family physician, a geriatric medicine specialist, and a psychiatrist, nowhere did anyone mention the connection between faith and health. In fact, one of my professors told me that religion often conflicted with medicine, and that religious beliefs were often held by those who were neurotic or otherwise unstable emotionally. As proof, he referred me to the book *Future of an Illusion*, the complete works of Dr. Sigmund Freud, known as the father of psychoanalysis.

However, as I began to practice medicine and see patients in a wide range of settings (from hospital to medical clinic), my experience with religious individuals didn't match what I had been taught. Those who were deeply religious were often the easiest and nicest patients to care for, were appreciative of the attention they received, and often coped remarkably well with complex and difficult medical problems. Patients without a religious faith or those who were angry with God proved the most difficult to care for and did not cope well with their illnesses.

Today there are hundreds—perhaps thousands—of studies published in peer-reviewed medical, nursing, public health, psychology, and psychiatric journals showing a connection between religious beliefs and behaviors and health. These studies have been reported by many different research groups in various academic institutions and in almost every country in the world. It is difficult to imagine that biased researchers either concocted all these studies to convince others or somehow got their findings mixed up.

Is religion good for your health? For most individuals, the answer is yes. Of course, there are certain groups that seem to espouse strong religious beliefs, but manipulate and distort religion to serve their personal agendas. Such approaches often involve the dominance and control of others, especially those who are vulnerable and uninformed. Groups such as ISIS and Boko Haram come to mind. However, this is not the kind of religion I'm discussing. I'm talking about faith that gives life meaning and purpose, and involves surrendering one's life to the divine as understood. This kind of religion balances loving God and loving neighbor.

Dr. Fleury's book is a good example of this balance. It provides an informative historical background, reviews existing scientific evidence, and offers solid advice on how to live one's life in a healthy manner—namely through a devout faith and behaviors that reflect that faith (including taking care of one's body as a temple of the Holy Spirit). It encourages the development of, and living out of, virtues that all healthy religions espouse.

Traits such as compassion, forgiveness, dependability, honesty, and respect for others—qualities especially emphasized in the Christian tradition. Dr. Fleury also reviews the importance of fasting and prayer, reading the Holy Scriptures, and actively participating in a faith community. This is a doctor talking here, not a priest or minister. There is plenty of science that backs up his words.

—HAROLD G. KOENIG, MD
Professor of Psychiatry and Behavioral Sciences
Associate Professor of Medicine
Director, Center for Spirituality, Theology, and Health
Duke University Medical Center, Durham, North Carolina;
Adjunct Professor, Department of Medicine,
King Abdulaziz University, Jeddah, Saudi Arabia;
and Adjunct Professor of Public Health,
Ningxia Medical University, Yinchuan, P. R. China
www.spiritualityandhealth.duke.edu

INTRODUCTION

T HE GOAL OF this work is not to stir up the old rivalry between science and faith. My aim is quite to the contrary! I want to summarize the current state of knowledge in a domain that increasingly calls into question the stance scientists and doctors hold toward faith. It is not the vocation of faith to make one renounce science and modernity, no more than science must become a religion.

In the medical field others have regularly questioned my dual role as a doctor and a believer—even more so as a pastor. They seemed to consider this a strange association that generates a type of "intellectual schizophrenia." In other words, can one reasonably be both a practicing believer and medical practitioner? Is it possible to be confident in the validity of the gospel in its plenitude—including divine healing—and still be at the forefront of cutting-edge scientific and medical knowledge? Whether one is a doctor or patient, can one legitimately accept faith and spirituality as a valid option to provide relief or healing? Do the answers fall under theology and a supposedly "irrational" faith? Or do scientific arguments exist? Is there evidence that one can qualify as irrefutable to legitimize a spiritual approach to general health and healing in particular?

Two decades ago several visionary doctors took on this problem, often attracting the mockery (even contempt) of the rest of the scientific community. Within this community there are always precursors. Because, as I wrote these words, this topic was a cover story in *Time* magazine. It is true that over those two decades doctors accumulated a considerable sum of evidence demonstrating the beneficial role of faith and spirituality on human health. And as early as in 1993 one of the authors of numerous studies and books in this field was declaring, "The choice between science and spirituality appears increasingly artificial today, even from a scientific perspective. It is now possible to tell a new story, one that allows science and spirituality to stand side by side in a complementary way, neither trying to usurp or eliminate the other."[1]

So what credit can one grant to what some now call the "faith factor"? Is the scientific proof satisfactory to validate a spiritual approach regarding health in general and of healing in particular? To this point, doctors have followed the principle of evidence-based medicine. Any therapeutic principle, to be validated and integrated into current medical practice, must have established irrefutable proof of its beneficial character and be readily available to doctors and patients. This degree of proof is obtained through comparative clinical studies performed on groups of patients, according to defined standards of effective treatment.

This allows doctors to assess, say, the advantage of a surgical technique in terms of reducing mortality, or the occurrence of complications based on its impact on a certain patient population, compared to a similar group of patients. The mass of information gathered—sometimes on several thousand cases—is analyzed statistically to evaluate whether a significant advantage emerges.

Other, more broad-based (known as epidemiological) studies allow health experts to determine factors that influence the health and illnesses of human populations. This detailed study of health events provides a basis for public health interventions. For instance, this is how we can identify cardiovascular risk factors or the development of certain cancers. Or, inversely, factors that allow for protection against disease. These are the kind of studies that allow the declaration "smoking kills" on cigarette packages, or that we should eat five servings of fruits and vegetables a day to protect us from various cancers. They also encourage us to habitually practice physical activity to have a healthy heart. It is only via this kind of controlled study and approved, peer-reviewed literature that results of these studies are published in prominent international medical journals and brought before the medical community.

So if one applies the principles governing modern medicine to faith and spirituality, can one manage to prove their effectiveness in terms of health and healing? Without question, the answer is yes.

I will only discuss aspects relative to Christian spirituality. I bring them to the table because this is the faith I practice and know from experience. In addition, it is also that which has been most observed in the United States. When applied to everyday life, the timeless spiritual values as passed down to us through Christ Himself appear to best correspond to those things required to lead a healthy and flourishing life. Current scientific findings demonstrate this truth.

This study owes much to the work of several doctors who were forerunners in this domain. They were men of science and faith, who risked compromising their careers and reputations in exploring this particular field. Notably, I think of my American honorable colleagues, doctors Harold Koenig, Dale Matthews, and Larry Dossey, and others who followed in their footsteps. Such pioneers interested themselves with their patients' bodies and their souls. I also think of Dr. Herbert Benson, professor at the prestigious Harvard Medical School and creator of the Benson-Henry Institute for Mind Body Medicine at Massachusetts General Hospital in Boston. Dr. Benson is one of the leading doctors of the modern era to place the relationship between mental states and physical health into evidence and to advocate for a medicine termed *integrative* because it takes into account patients' beliefs. These courageous pioneers deserve thanks for their contribution to the progress of medicine and pursuit of its goal: to improve the health and well-being of human beings.

My goal is to encourage you to put your confidence in God regarding health and healing. If you are religious, you have an excellent reason to believe in them and to deepen your faith. Obviously there are theological reasons, but I hope to persuade you there are also scientific factors that support this view.

In any case the many benefits noted within these pages about spirituality means there is more to good health than simply asking for a doctor's opinion. I hope you will glean understanding and also become an advocate of the view that spirituality and modern medicine can join forces for the benefit of patients.

—DR. MAX FLEURY
Orléans, France

CHAPTER 1

FAITH AND HEALING: A CONTINUOUS TRADITION

Is anyone among you suffering? Let him pray. Is anyone merry? Let him sing psalms. Is anyone sick among you? Let him call for the elders of the church, and let them pray over him, anointing him with oil in the name of the Lord. And the prayer of faith will save the sick, and the Lord will raise him up. And if he has committed any sins, he will be forgiven.

—JAMES 5:13-15

AROUND THE YEAR AD 60 this was how the Apostle James exhorted members of first-century Christian communities to deal with sickness. Since the beginning of time healing from illness has preoccupied countless numbers of people. Faith and religious practice brought a response to this concern. For thousands of years—whether for themselves, friends, or loved ones—humans have prayed for healing. Sacred history overflows with stories of inexplicable recoveries from sickness and disease. Yet the unbelievable nature of these accounts, which rely on faith rather than reason, have created considerable conflict between science and religion. Public scorn for the other camp characterizes their exchanges.

Despite this situation, it appears that those upholding each view are on the cusp of finding common ground. Increasing numbers of scientists are demonstrating interest in cures that medicine does not—or cannot— explain in hopes of unraveling the mystery. Outside of extraordinary cases, does religious practice bring certain health benefits? All around the world, and particularly in the United States, a multiplying number of scientific studies are seeking to analyze the benefits of spirituality to healing.

Once practiced almost exclusively by Pentecostal Christians, healing prayer is attracting increasing interest. That includes believers from more traditional spiritual environments, whether Catholic or Protestant. Only a few decades ago one commonly heard certain preachers assert that God "permitted" us to be stricken by some illness in order to test or chastise us. Yet nothing in Scripture allows for such an idea! Nor does the theory that Paul's famous thorn in the flesh is part of the communion of Christ's sufferings. (See 2 Corinthians 12:7; Philippians 3:10.) Relating a few isolated passages to illness, or the idea that physical suffering permits our ascension to heaven, is an abuse of sound scriptural interpretation. Explore the

New Testament and you will see that Jesus went about healing everyone He touched. Examples span from blind Bartimaeus, to the woman with an issue of blood, to the daughter of Jairus (the ruler of the synagogue), to the Roman centurion's servant, to the anonymous multitudes that He met during His travels. Scripture indicates that He healed all kinds of sicknesses and diseases (Matt. 4:23).

After Jesus ascended to heaven, His disciples put His word into practice, buoyed by this promise: "He who believes in Me will do the works that I do also. And he will do greater works than these, because I am going to My Father" (John 14:12). In that vein Peter and John healed a lame man at the gate of the Temple of Jerusalem (Acts 3). The apostles prayed to the Lord: "Show your power by healing, performing miracles, and doing amazing things through the power and the name of your holy servant Jesus" (Acts 4:30, GW). Three verses later that is what He did! In Samaria Philip performed miracles and healed many paralyzed and lame persons (Acts 8:7–8). Not surprisingly this resulted in great joy among the people.

PEACE AND JOY

Later the Apostle Paul taught the Roman Christians that the kingdom of God is not found in eating and drinking but in righteousness, peace, and joy in the Holy Spirit (Rom. 14:17). Indeed, what is more wrongful than an illness? What threatens peace and joy more than serious health problems? Healing from sickness restores peace and righteousness and produces joy, as Philip's adventures in Samaria proved.

In Lydda, Peter healed a paralytic by repeating, nearly verbatim, the words Jesus used in healing the sick (Acts 9:33). A bit later in Jaffa, Peter revived Tabitha—who had been deceased. That is powerful healing! Paul performed a number of miracles after his conversion, as reported in Acts: "God was performing extraordinary miracles by the hands of Paul, so that handkerchiefs or aprons were even carried from his body to the sick, and the diseases left them and the evil spirits went out" (Acts 19:11–12, NAS). After Publius's father came down with dysentery in Malta, Paul prayed for him by laying his hands upon him and healing him, just as with other illnesses presented to Paul on the island (Acts 28). A closer look at the Book of Acts shows that prior to healing, all the apostles announced the gospel and proclaimed the salvation and remission of sins in Jesus Christ. Such preaching stirred numerous miraculous signs, including healing.

Contrary to the idea pushed by cessationists who teach that miracles disappeared after the death of the first apostles, miraculous healings carried on within the early church and later, most notably through the Desert Fathers. These hermits lived in the deserts of Egypt and the Middle East in the third century and perpetuated the apostolic tradition. However, little by little the purity of this tradition became perverted through magic or superstitious practices. While lack of sound teaching had something to do with this, it also stemmed from the institutionalization of the church.

Sadly unethical spiritual leaders used their position to pressure and manipulate the gullible masses. As early as the beginning of the Middle Ages questionable and corruptible practices supplanted the veritable ministry of healing in the institutional church. A few centuries later the disappearance of the healing gift benefited such supporters of "enlightened" rationalism as the French philosopher Voltaire. Ironically, although Protestants took an opposite approach to the institutionalized church, reformers such as Luther and John Calvin contributed to this disconnect of God from people's daily lives by rejecting any "supernatural" aspects of His activity.

In *Quenching the Spirit* William DeArtega could not be clearer: "In Reformed theology, no present-day spiritual experiences such as visions or prophecies would be of the Lord, so that such experiences were either delusion (enthusiasm) or entrapments of the devil.... The tragedy of Calvin's attempt to reform medieval Catholicism was that in negating Catholic quasi-Gnosticism (the overestimation of spiritual experiences), he fell into quasi-Pharisaism (the premature rejection of most spiritual experiences)."[1]

HEALING CONTINUES

Despite everything, the ministry of healing continued to manifest itself throughout church history. However, one cannot rely on the "official" version of church history to discover the evidence. Since periods of awakening occurred during the evolution of the church, one

5

must understand a return to spirituality and the simplicity of primitive Christianity experienced by certain communities. This almost always accompanied a resurgence of the "charisms" of power, namely, healing, deliverance (exorcism), and mass conversions. These awakenings usually ended by burning themselves out—without a doubt, victims of what they opposed, the institutionalization of faith. The most recent embodiment, the Pentecostal revival, started at a small Bible school in Kansas in 1901. It flared into international prominence five years later at 321 Azusa Street in Los Angeles. Continuing today, the Azusa Street Revival reemphasized healing through faith and prayer with the laying on of hands.

Whether called Pentecostalism among Evangelical Protestants or Charismatic renewal in the Catholic Church, this movement constitutes the number-one force within the church. Its followers number more than five hundred million worldwide and many rapidly growing communities. In China alone the number of Pentecostal Christians is estimated at fifty million. Fought at first by the churches from which they sprang, Charismatics and Pentecostals continued on their path and managed to win some over with their practices. The Charismatic renewal is largely recognized within Catholic circles and constitutes a breeding ground for new priests.

The movement is gaining ground in Protestant circles too. A prime example is my country of France, where more than half of the Baptist churches are of Charismatic expression; Charismatics (including

pastors) are part of Reformed and Lutheran congrega-
tions. As a result, praying for the sick is no longer considered strange, nor is healing prayer reserved for those
who have the luck (or courage) to attend a Pentecostal
meeting. It has reached into the heart of middle-class
homes and touched the members of mainstream
denominations that—figuratively speaking—not long
ago would have fled, horrified at the idea of anyone
laying hands on them!

Guy Jalbert, a Catholic priest from Quebec who
authored *Priez afin que vous soyez guéris* (Pray so that
you may be healed), noted, "The Church must continue
the ministry of Jesus's compassion and healing: 'They
will lay hands on the sick and these will be healed.'
Healing the sick is a task that is incumbent upon the
Church."[2] Jalbert observed that the Greek fathers, the
theologians of the Church's first centuries of existence, left us a theology of healing—presenting Jesus as
the Messiah who saved us *and* a doctor who heals us.
According to this theology, Adam lived in a primor-
dial state of health before his sin, adorned with every
virtue. Through original sin, he lost this state of health
for himself and his descendants, leaving him and all
who followed susceptible to all sorts of illnesses. This
condemned the human race to a physical and a spiritual death.

Despite this situation, the Bible illustrates a God who
wants to heal our illnesses. This is why He sent His
Son to be our supreme physician. "Humanity needed
a doctor and a surgeon whose skill was proportionate
to the importance of its illnesses and of its wounds,"

wrote Jean Climaque, a Syrian monk in the sixth and seventh centuries who retired to Mount Sinai for more than sixty years—as cited by Jean-Claude Larchet in his book *Thérapeutique des maladies spirituelles* (Therapeutics of spiritual illnesses).[3]

A respected theological in the early church, Cyril of Jerusalem, also pointed out that the name of Jesus means Savior, but that in Greek it also means doctor: "You shall call His name JESUS, for *He will save* His people from their sins." (Matt. 1:21, emphasis added). The Greek word for save is *sozo*, which also means to be delivered or shielded from peril. It appears fourteen times in the Gospels to designate a physical healing, and twenty times to designate the salvation of life threatened by danger or imminent death. Elsewhere, the third-century theologian Origen presented the parable of the Good Samaritan as a representation of Christ the doctor.

SEPARATION OF CHURCH AND MEDICINE

In the West medicine and religion were closely aligned until the end of the Middle Ages. Religious orders founded hospices (often called hostels of God), often building them in the shadow of cathedrals or monasteries. Hence the church pervaded the practice of medicine. Doctors and nurses usually came from the ranks of the clergy, as did the herbalists who cultivated and prescribed medicinal plants. Yet the scientific revolution, initiated in the seventeenth century, spelled the end of this marriage of love and reason. "Rational thinkers" steered Western medicine toward what it has become today.

In 1637 a French philosopher and mathematician from Touraine went down in history by publishing his *Discourse on the Method*. René Descartes involuntarily gave rise to Cartesianism and a multitude of disciples who took up his theses and simplified them to the extreme—in every sense of the word. The misguided condemnation of Galileo in 1633 by the Catholic Church appeared to trigger the writing and publication of Descartes's famous work. Repulsed by the church's action, Descartes wanted to substitute the Middle Age's uncertain faith practices with a science whose certitude equaled that of mathematics. He wanted to use practical applications of science that allowed men to be "like masters and possessors of nature."[4] In his eyes humans could attain a universal knowledge through reason and by using all the resources of his intelligence. His legendary statement, "I think, therefore I am," is known widely in the academy and beyond. It summarizes Descartes's philosophy that humans are a thinking substance. Without resorting to faith, he suggested that they can rely on reason alone to attain knowledge.

In biology, as in physics, Descartes stood against the idea of hidden forces in nature. As so many Enlightenment thinkers did, he reasoned that everything can be explained through space and movement. There is nothing more to living than in the automatons he observed in the king's gardens. In *Discourse on Method, Part V* Descartes wrote that animals are obedient to their urges, meaning they follow the principle of causality—meaning that under identical conditions, the same causes produce the same effects. Since an external stimulus produces a predictable behavioral response in an animal, he theorized that one day people could conceive a machine that would be indistinguishable from a real animal.

Born in 1709 Dr. Julien Offray de La Mettrie appropriated and amplified Descartes's ideas. An atheist and libertine, Mettrie expounded on the idea of a radical materialism. In 1745 he wrote *L'histoire naturelle de l'âme* (The natural history of the soul), in which he promoted his thesis that the mind must be recognized as a consequence of the sophisticated organization of the human brain. Man is thus only a superior animal. Later his *L'homme—machine* (Man a machine) extended Descartes's principles to human beings while soundly rejecting the idea of God.

The scientific revolution that sprang first from Nicolaus Copernicus (who preceded Descartes by a century) and then Descartes's ideas continues to this day. The majority of Western doctors are trained in this school of thought. While allowing for remarkable advances, it has reached its human limits. Led to reason only in respect to that which is observable, measurable, and reproducible in laboratory situations, these practitioners perpetuate the concepts of *L'homme—machine*. The problem is how this philosophy reduces the complex human being to a simple collection of organs. The predictable result: most modern doctors restrict their interest to the physical body and ailments expressed through clinical or biological symptoms. Then they treat the abnormality, all the while overlooking the spiritual causes or implications of the ailment. The care of the soul is left to the specialists of the psyche—the psychologists, psychotherapists, and psychiatrists. Like all doctors, they search for physical symptoms and ignore spiritual ones. This unbalanced situation leaves out the fathers, pastors, priests, and counselors who care for the spirit.

THE REBIRTH OF SPIRITUALITY IN MEDICINE

In his eponymous 2008 book *La Maladie a-t-elle un Sens?* (Does sickness have a meaning?) former surgeon turned psychotherapist Thierry Janssen posed the question of whether sickness has meaning: "It's a question that concerns all of us. Even though medicine no longer poses it to itself. Indeed, it tends to the body without being concerned about the entirety of the human person. By prioritizing the understanding of details, it forgets the ties which unite the patients of the world in which we live."[5]

If we are called to search for the real meaning of sickness and its multiple factors, logic says we are also called to think about the real meaning of healing. Could it be considered simply as the restoration of health? The only problem with this is that a state of absolute health does not exist. All complex biological organisms experience structural problems, stemming from various dysfunctions.

Healing, then, should not be considered the restoration of absolute health, but a return to an "optimum" physiological state. This can occur through several factors, be they natural (the body's own defenses), medical (medications and medical/surgical procedures), or spiritual (personal beliefs and communities of faith). This third element of healing forces us to examine whether there is a relationship between spiritual factors and other forms of healing. And if we can believe in divine healing from a theological point of view, what are the implications for a scientific point of view? If we apply the methods of investigation behind evidence-based medicine to prayer and spirituality, we are able to bring forth a clear, objective response—in the affirmative.

If one considers the growing body of scientific evidence on the subject, Descartes would probably be the first to agree that an active spiritual life can benefit one's health. I can envision him encouraging members of the medical profession to take this dimension of their patients into account, since it constitutes a powerful factor. In many cases today an increasing number of specialists interest themselves with the question— outside personal religious convictions. At the time of this writing specialists in functional neuroimaging (techniques such as functional MRI allow them to literally "see" brain functioning) were taking a passionate interest in the topic. Such experts are publishing scientific papers on the modifications of cerebral functioning during prayer or on the benefits of meditation in terms of improving cognitive functions. In the December 12, 2007 issue of *The American Journal of*

Psychiatry Dr. Burr Eichelmann wondered, "Are we training our profession sufficiently in the language and concepts of religion and spirituality?"[6] He was referring to an investigation published in that edition that highlighted that psychiatrists—similar to other medical doctors—were unanimous in recognizing the benefits of religion and spirituality on health.

Among other voices that recognize such benefits is Dr. Dale Matthews, who practices general internal medicine in McLean, Virginia, and is a staff physician in the Primary Care Division of the Virginia Hospital Center Physician Group, based in Arlington. He is the author of a four-volume research work titled *The Faith Factor: An Annotated Bibliography of Clinical Research on Spiritual Subjects*, which gathered studies published on this topic. They had been published in such prestigious medical journals as *The American Journal of Public Health, Cancer, The American Journal of Psychiatry*, and many others. The spiritual implications of this exhaustive analysis are astonishing. While such factors as socioeconomic levels, eating habits, and physical activity play important roles in health, the spiritual dimension—this famous faith factor—appears to far exceed others. Its benefits appear to extend to all ages and all aspects of health, from disease prevention to healing.

In 1999 Dr. Matthews released the general public version of *The Faith Factor*. In it he noted spirituality is an important element in his medical practice: "It began to make logical sense to me that, as a proponent of true, whole-person medicine and as a person of faith seeking to live out my faith in a life of service to others, I should, and could, address all my patients' principal needs-physical, psychological, social, and spiritual"[7] Certain patients seek help from Dr. Matthews because of his stance on faith—in addition to his excellent professional reputation. During initial conversations with patients, he asks about their relationship with God. If a patient is a churchgoer, he may ask more about that. When he prescribes a medication, he will add an appropriate Bible verse and offer to pray. However, if the patient is not receptive he doesn't insist.

THE NEED FOR HOLISTIC CARE

In addition to books such as *The Faith Factor*, a landmark reference work appeared in 2001. *The Handbook of Religion and Health* was written by Harold Koenig, Michael McCullough, and David Larson. (The second edition, released in 2012, was coauthored by Harold Koenig, Dana King, and Verna Benner Carlson.) This twelve hundred-page manual reviews more than three thousand published and unpublished studies undertaken since 1900, along with verifying their scientific rigor. Once again, these reveal that spiritual activities positively affect life's quality and longevity.

Dr. Koenig, who has written eighteen books about the relationship between religion and health, sees three fundamental explanations for the medical profession's interest in this topic.

First, there is a growing role of religion and spirituality in people's lives. Against all odds, and despite the fact that we live in an increasingly secular society, one is indeed witness to a revival of faith—even among young people. A primary reason is how the modern world's materialistic and hedonistic values fail to speak to individuals' deep spiritual longings and aspirations. Nor do they offer suitable responses to the world's increasingly perplexing problems. Consider the phenomenal worldwide success of such material as the Alpha course; or books such as Rick Warren's *The Purpose-Driven Life*, which sold more than thirty million copies sold; or *The Shack* by Paul Young, a novel originally self-published and so successful the author sold the publishing rights to an international firm. Despite the problems confronting religious institutions in a changing world, as we progress into the twenty-first century we are witnessing a widespread return of religious sentiment. This has consequences for the health of countless numbers of people.

Second, the economic and demographic trends driving health expenditures are higher. At a time when the age pyramid is in the middle of turning on its head due to aging demographics, active spirituality could help prevent the onset of chronic conditions and mental illnesses, and reduce costs associated with medical expenditures and lost work hours. Furthermore, community involvement makes it possible to overcome isolation and maintain social cohesiveness in our fragmented societies.

Third, there is an ongoing crisis in medicine itself. Modern medicine's overspecialized approach has created a shortage of general practitioners. Not only does this make access to health care increasingly difficult, an overall reduction in government and insurance reimbursements has forced people to delay necessary treatment or prescriptions. Such trends combine to create a sense of malaise among patients—the feeling they are little more than "one more body" in the system or that their identity has been reduced to a set of symptoms. I notice this daily in my medical practice: patients need us to talk with them, explain our jargon in terms they can understand, and show them empathy. They crave a doctor who looks beneath the surface symptoms that brought them to our office. The introduction of a spiritual dimension in the doctor-patient relationship will allow for a holistic approach that treats the whole person.

Sadly for much of the profession it is incongruous to discuss incorporating faith into a medical practice, let alone propose that a doctor consider praying for a patient. Too many doctors are anchored to a mechanistic tradition of health and healing whose roots only go back a few centuries. It is time to shed our *enlightened* outlook and admit the truth that the body and spirit are one. In the past the two had been considered as such and deserved to be treated as a whole. In the end our patients will be healthier—and happier.

CHAPTER 2

HOW FAITH REDUCES STRESS

Happy is he who has the God of Jacob for
his help, whose hope is in the LORD God.

—PSALM 146:5, JUB

T HE ROLE OF spirituality in health is typically a
source of debate between supporters and detrac-
tors. Yet research shows many patients are already sold
on the idea. US medical researchers have extensively
studied the topic of coping—the personal capacity to
confront a difficult situation and deal with the consequences. Such studies report than in states with the
largest percentage of practicing believers, between
33 and 50 percent of patients cited their faith as the
most common means of fighting the stress brought
on by illness.

Those who suffer from chronic diseases or serious illnesses are best suited to verify the role of the role of faith and prayer in the battle against adversity. Faith and spirituality are essential for followers of Christ. Their beliefs make it possible to find a reason for existence that is sorely missing today from too many people's lives. For these believers faith creates a heightened feeling of well-being and a better quality of life. Contrary to the preconceived notions that create an image of practicing Christians as inhibited or frustrated, studies show they are much happier than nonbelievers. Also, contrary to popular images, they are more enthusiastic about life and have a greater sense of accomplishment than atheists, agnostics, and other skeptics.

Studies affirming this have existed for many years. One study published in 1984 examined the relationship between religious activities and feelings of well-being among participants. Researchers asked them to evaluate their level of satisfaction. The results showed that joy, enthusiasm, and levels of satisfaction with life correlated to the frequency of participation in community and religious activities. Another study released in 1988 reviewed a forty-year-long survey of 1,650 individuals. It revealed that regular church attenders report a much higher level of overall satisfaction with life. They also benefited from a significantly higher percentage of "happy" marriages than the general population.

This link between faith and quality of life is even more evident in older persons, as seen by a survey of nearly one thousand women (married or widowed) between the ages of sixty and sixty-five. The study evaluated their levels of health, religious practice, and fertility to evaluate these factors on their overall satisfaction in life. Among the participants the level of religious practice was the most reliable indicator of satisfaction. Among widows the level of spirituality closely correlated to their feelings of general well-being.

The same trends exist among youth. A survey of students at the University of Western Ontario highlighted that those who attended a Christian group on campus had better morale as a whole, significantly lower levels of stress, and a better level of health (i.e., fewer visits to a nurse, doctor, or dentist) than those who didn't attend such groups.

Personal Devotion

Numerous surveys, such as those I just cited, evaluate religious practice through attendance at a traditional church or meetings of a religious group. However, what about the quality of personal devotion—what we might label the "private" practice of belief? Is it also a factor? The answer is yes. In terms of well-being and satisfaction with life, individuals who practice an intrinsic spirituality appear to enjoy the greatest benefits.

Professor Margaret Poloma, a sociologist of religion at the University of Akron in Ohio, studied the quality of life of religious and practicing individuals. Poloma surveyed the level of a subject's well-being, both through participation in communal activities and personal spiritual practices. Those who used a natural or meditative form of prayer reported the highest level of spiritual satisfaction and overall well-being. On the other hand, subjects who relied on ritualistic forms of prayer showed a lower satisfaction with life and lower feelings of well-being. This tends to show that the benefits an individual takes away from his or her spirituality depend on the level of involvement in community activities, personal devotional life, and the person's concept of God.

Regular participation in a church or spiritual group makes a difference. Those who are part of a group that eagerly embraces the value of prayer are more likely to make prayer a part of daily life outside of church. An individual's concept of God appears to make an even bigger impact on one's outlook. If a person sees God as a big boss pulling strings arbitrarily, will consider prayer as a mystery that escapes human reason, or thinks that God only works through some kind of formula, he or she is less likely to experience the profound joy that comes from a sense of closeness with God. Such a person is also less inclined to see God as a partner or friend.

Christopher Ellison, a professor of sociology at the University of Texas, identified such trends in his studies. His work showed that joy and satisfaction related not just to participation in church activities, but also to one's feeling of closeness to God. Those who devoted themselves to prayer and other spiritual activities in daily life, as well as attending church, reaped the rewards. However, those who attended their church or parish out of a sense of duty and had little concept out-side of services derived fewer personal benefits.

Given that our relationship with God depends on our view of Him, it is evident that subjects who con-sider God as good and compassionate are more likely to develop an intimate spirituality and see the greatest benefits. Contrary to the widespread image of prac-ticing believers as more neurotic than nonbelievers, Ellison's study demonstrated the opposite. The survey participants who saw God as a loving and compas-sionate being reported lesser feelings of solitude and greater joy of living than those who see God as a severe, vengeful being.

The benefits of a devoted spiritual life and faith become crucial when serious or life-threatening dis-eases strike. To objectively evaluate this benefit, one must identify a group of patients who suffer from a serious and prolonged disease. The creation of the stress that often accompanies chronic illness means the patient must find ways to adapt. Some examples are elderly persons who experience isolation or mul-tiple illnesses that diminish their mental and physical capabilities, or patients who suffer from costly ill-nesses that require skilled nursing care and expensive medical treatments—such as people with an advanced stage of cancer.

Having defined the population of interest, one must next evaluate the importance of faith as a coping mechanism. The simplest way is to pose an open-ended question, asking patients what allows them to endure anxiety, pain, or handicaps. This method has a disadvantage; it can underestimate the impact of religion. This is especially true if a patient feels inhibited about speaking openly about spirituality with a doctor. Another method is to ask the patient to select the most effective method from a list of support strategies. A third consists of directly questioning the patient on the subject of faith and religion.

ALLEVIATING BURDENS

Thanks to these methods, researchers have studied the role of religion and spirituality in patients suffering from a variety of illnesses, such as kidney failure, cancer, cardiovascular diseases, AIDS, and diabetes. These studies show mixed results, according to the methods used to question the patients (as outlined earlier). Overall it is possible to assert that recourse to religion to confront costly illnesses is widespread, particularly among the elderly. This reliance on spirituality increases with the seriousness of the condition or the level of stress. This is indicative of the fact that the more substantial the stress, or the more unfavorable the prognosis, the more the patient calls on his or her faith resources to alleviate burdens.

In 1990 a study completed in the Midwest by Kenneth Pargament highlighted the aspects of spirituality that appeared the most suitable to help people confront disease:

- Faith in a just and loving God

   Again, the conception that the subject had of God appeared to be essential to finding comfort despite the problems associated with the disease. The person who only saw the Almighty as one who judges and punishes found less help in his or her distress.

- The experience that God is truly on our side in distress

   If God really loves us and takes care of us, then it is possible to experience His help in times of distress, like a "presence" that does not desert us. To the contrary, the patient who did not have this notion of a close God, but instead saw Him as a kind of impersonal great watchmaker, did not experience this comfort.

- Involvement in religious rituals

   This concerns participation in routine liturgical activities. The study showed how the repetition of gestures or activities—what some might term "rituals"—brought people relief by means of the activation of certain regions of the brain. People in the spotlight, such as high-performance athletes or Broadway performers, follow rituals to get rid of stress. Then there are those with obsessive-compulsive disorders; without rituals pathologically anxious patients could not live. In this study religious rituals brought to believers the same relaxing and anxiolytic effect that is particularly precious to others undergoing periods of great stress.

- The personal and active pursuit of help in spirituality
Those who actively sought help in spirituality had the highest probability of effectively finding this comfort.[1] It may seem obvious at first sight, but this is oddly reminiscent of the words Jesus addressed to His disciples: "Ask and it will be given to you; seek and you will find; knock and it will be opened to you" (Matt. 7:7).

In putting these different mechanisms into place, patients who prayed and involved spirituality in their fight against disease also displayed the greatest resilience. They succumbed the least to feelings of despair that often accompany a long-term illness. The effectiveness of faith as support when a serious illness strikes is not surprising, since it represents not only a physical trial, but also a psychological and spiritual test. As Dr. Matthews noted in *The Faith Factor*: "As long as we are well, we can remain relatively independent, and we gain feelings of self-worth and purpose from our work in the world, from our role in the family, and from our hobbies and volunteer activities. Once serious illness strikes, some of all these sources of satisfaction may be blocked. We can no longer derive our self-esteem from our accomplishments; we may no longer be able to care for our own bodies. For most people, serious illness provokes a re-evaluation of life's meaning and purpose. For many it causes a radical reversal of life-style."[2] As long as you are well, you can remain relatively independent, and you find your reason to live in your work, in your role in society, in the family, your leisure or associative hobbies.

THE VALUE OF FAITH

This tendency in the most severely affected patients can be transitory and due precisely to the difficult circumstances with which they must cope. The adage says it well: "There are no atheists in foxholes." However, to determine the importance of religious belief, it is necessary to question the overall population—not just patients. In a recent survey by the Gallup Organization, 78 percent of respondents said that religion was "very important" or "fairly important" in their lives.[3] This finding confirms long-term trends. Twenty-five years earlier the same percentage agreed that their beliefs were a source of comfort and support. A study in 1999 by the Religion Research Center at Princeton University showed that when it comes to facing difficulties—contrary to what prevailing secularists would like us to believe—personal faith holds an important place in the majority of American citizens' lives.

Faith and prayer are not only valuable support for patients, but also for those taking care of them. In particular this affects caretakers for people suffering from Alzheimer's disease or various forms of cancers, and the parents of children with a chronic illness. Caring for a seriously ill loved one is a source of chronic stress, which can be the source of anxiety, depression, or an increased risk of physical illness.

One of the first studies highlighting the benefits of faith in those close to patients affected by Alzheimer's disease took place in 1984. Seventy-four percent of family members questioned identified prayer as their first aid in dealing with distress brought about by a parent's illness. Another study the following year showed that the burden caused by serious disease of a loved one is inversely proportional to the importance accorded to faith and spirituality. A 1994 study looked at the benefits of spirituality for those close to Alzheimer's patients. This survey highlighted how regular participation in religious activities and the degree of spiritual satisfaction were inversely proportional to the risk of developing chronic stress. This participation also promoted continuing feelings of social inclusion.

Other studies have reviewed Christian and non-Christian caregivers for patients suffering from advanced or terminal cancers. They concluded that a solid faith and maintaining of social ties (through various religious community activities) were the most effective factors of adapting when a person faced the disease or disability of a loved one.

What about the loss of someone dear, such as the death of a child? Several studies have shown the effectiveness of faith when it comes to enduring grief. Kenneth Maton, a psychologist at the University of Maryland, studied the behavior of parents who had lost a child to analyze the effectiveness of spirituality in coping with this emotional catastrophe. Maton's study showed significant value of religious beliefs in the panoply of options available to parents. While the study showed the importance of conversation and sharing groups, it also revealed that the parents who also found spiritual support (prayer groups, community sharing) suffered the lowest incidence of depression.

However, researchers have taken more than attendance at a church or religious community into account. Another study of 139 people who had lost their spouses evaluated their level of depression and religious orientation, whether intrinsic or extrinsic. Again, as with previous studies, this orientation made a difference. Subjects having an extrinsic spirituality— namely, one more oriented at an institution than a closely held personal belief—suffered more from depression and feelings of despair than those with an intrinsic spiritual orientation. Taking these elements into account shows how people in deep mourning need to not only take care of their physical and psychological health but also should be encouraged by doctors to develop a genuine, personal spirituality and attend religious services regularly.

LEANING ON GOD

It is interesting to note that these effects vary by more than a personal degree of religious involvement. It also involves an individual's interpretation of events, according to his or her theological understanding. The utilization of questionnaires allow researchers to evaluate the degree of lingering resentment within individuals who have dealt with serious loss, or to the benefit they derived from leaning on God to confront life's difficulties. Other scales allow for the measurement of mental stability from the level of self-esteem, anxiety, and psychosocial competence—in other words, the capacity to adequately resolve problems.

In reviewing such evaluations, it is remarkable that people who are apathetic about religion, have a tendency to rely on oneself, or doubt the very existence of God, show the worst scores for mental stability. By contrast, what many psychologists term as "religious denial" relates to a positive mental state. Researchers rate as "religious denial" those who agree with such statements as, "I believe that this hardship brings me closer to God," "I'm holding in there because I'm sure that it is God's will that I go through it," or "I believe that God's plans are always perfect."

Despite these psychologists' views, the conclusion from examining numerous objective studies is that a strong faith, active religious practice, and attendance at a spiritual community is a plus when facing a major crisis. This plus can be objectively measured in terms of quality of life and adaptation to stress. This confidence in God is also, as I will review in coming chapters, a healing factor.

So what should the role of physicians be in all of this? Is it necessary that they involve themselves in the spirituality of their patients? Again, numerous US studies examined patients and the overall population. These surveys revealed that—for the most part—patients found it important and comforting that their doctor preoccupies himself (or herself) with their spiritual state. Ironically, although religious practice is widespread in the US and it is normal to express one's beliefs, it is American doctors who appear reluctant to embrace this reality. This is where more physicians need to appreciate the limitations their scientific training and Western rationalism has placed on them. By failing to see the value faith plays in increasing millions of people's health and satisfaction with life, they are doing their patients a major disservice.

CHAPTER 3

HEALTHY IS THE LORD!

My son, do not forget my teaching, but let your
heart keep my commandments; for length of days
and long life and peace will they add to you....It will
be health to your body, and strength to your bones.

—PROVERBS 3:1-2, 8

T HE BEST WAY to maintain health sounds too
obvious: to remain in a healthy state and not suc-
cumb to illness. Yet today we know that when it comes
to the most widespread diseases, many are linked to
risk factors that promote their outbreak. They include
such problems as cardiovascular diseases, cancer, diabetes, certain infectious diseases, and even some
mental illness. In most cases the risk factors are linked
to a person's behavior. When it comes to the habits we
follow—i.e., the food we eat and the exercise (or lack of)
we get—the things we do will either harm our health
or improve it.

Among poor habits adversely affecting health is the ingestion of toxins. Smoking is notably responsible for cardiovascular problems, cancers, and respiratory diseases. Next comes alcohol; overconsumption promotes certain cancers, digestive diseases, and mental problems. Finally, consumption of a diverse assortment of addictive substances is widespread, whether marijuana, cocaine, heroin, or other substances—especially opioids. These promote psychological or psychiatric disorders, the transmission of such infectious diseases as AIDS or hepatitis, and hazardous behaviors.

Aside from consuming such toxins, a poor lifestyle promotes health problems. These include such factors as physical inactivity, excessive consumption of calories (commonly called overeating), unsafe sexual practices, insufficient sleep, and chronic stress. All major religions encourage a healthy lifestyle, with many prohibiting the consumption of various toxins. Hindus and Buddhists are generally vegetarians, while Jews and Muslims also embrace strict dietary rules. All established religions explicitly forbid or discourage the abuse of alcohol, unsafe sexual practices, and other behaviors that can put the body in danger of damage or disease. The Apostle Paul routinely denounced drunkenness, excessive eating, and other bad habits. In his first epistle the Apostle Peter spoke against past practices that converts engaged in prior to their decision to follow Christ, "when we walked in immorality: lusts, drunkenness, carousing, debauchery, and abominable idolatries" (1 Pet. 4:3).

A growing number of studies reveal that religious and practicing individuals enjoy a better state of health than the general public. Surveys of young people are particularly impressive. Those who are active in a Christian community and pray and read the Bible regularly are less inclined to smoke, drink alcohol, consume drugs, or indulge in unsafe behaviors than their peers. They are also less likely to engage in premarital sexual relations—which obviously offers the best protection against sexually transmitted diseases! These benefits continue into adult life. Religious practices constitute an effective defense against a poor lifestyle and ensuing health problems.

It appears that many high-risk, unsanitary behaviors stem from a profound discontentment with life, including disruptions caused by a dysfunctional family or social environment. Spirituality can serve as a counterbalance to the disappointments and rigors of this life. The subject who embraces personal faith practices, participates in a structured congregation, and follows wise guidelines will be less likely to seek comfort in excessive substances or behavior. Moreover, the social ties of a faith community create affection, benevolent feelings, and mutual respect, which allows people to avoid the problems that often accompany social isolation. If a regular participant no longer shows up to meetings, members often communicate with the absentee to see if anything is wrong. This can allow for early detection of a physical or psychological problem and lead to preventive steps before the damage is too great.

THE REALITY OF CONVERSION

For those who come to faith while dealing with addictions, conversion is sometimes accompanied by a remarkable deliverance. After all, conversion (*metanoia* in Greek) means the kind of turnaround that leads to a radical life change. Thus, those who experience a dramatic spiritual encounter often describe their desire to drink or consume drugs disappearing overnight, as if it had been removed by an outside force. While medical practitioners remain relatively powerless to explain such phenomena, they are nevertheless very real.

Many of us may know of men or women in faith communities who have experienced a profound change and are suddenly freed of the physical, emotional, or spiritual ties that kept them bound in problems. Some testify to a sort of "outside force" seizing them. Others describe the sudden filling of peace and joy. Others tell of an internal sense that they no longer needed toxins to relieve their stress. This is reminiscent of Jesus's words, delivered in the synagogue of Nazareth at the start of His ministry: "The Spirit of the Lord is upon Me, because He has anointed Me to preach the gospel to the poor; He has sent Me to heal the brokenhearted, to preach deliverance to the captives" (Luke 4:18). While skeptics regularly mock conversion experiences, such accounts are buttressed by the reality of changed lives. The overwhelming power of addictions is well established at both behavioral and biological levels. Something powerful *had to have occurred* in the lives of people for them to undergo transformations after years of pain and slavery.

Sometimes the change is less spectacular and more gradual, but leads to similar benefits. It is surprising that these realities go largely unsung—even deliberately ignored—by those whose stated goal (even profession) is helping drug addicts.

One of the first studies published in this field was released at the end of the 1970s. The National Institute on Drug Abuse carried out this study on a population of heroin addicts. Its principal investigator, David Desmond of San Antonio's University of Texas Health Science Center, followed a group of male heroin addicts. After treatment some joined a church that offered a support group for addicts that included prayer. After one year the patients who attended these groups displayed a rate of abstinence eight times higher than those who only utilized a secular follow-up program.

From a purely medical point of view, those who embrace faith likely benefit from a neuropsychological effect of their practices, such as prayer or contemplative Bible reading. Their mood improves as their stress level reduces. Both processes have a connection with the level of neurotransmitters in the brain—particularly serotonin. The relevance: a number of persons who are "naturally" anxious or depressive suffer from a cerebral lack of serotonin. In such a state people are predisposed to the abuse of toxic substances as they try to find peace. This is why a spiritual focus can prove so beneficial, since patients who follow this path often sense an absence (or fewer) of the cravings that controlled their past existence. They are under better emotional control; those who once used drugs to reduce anxiety no longer feel that life is out of control. An intense spiritual experience—like that of the Apostle Paul on the road to Damascus—often results in a radical life change.

OPIUM OR OPTIMISM?

Is religion the "opiate of the masses" that Karl Marx— the father of socialism—so heartily denounced? Through encouraging a spiritual practice, does one propose the replacing of one addiction by another? As a physician I have witnessed the physical, social, personal, and familial disasters caused by patients' alcoholism and drug addiction. If one adds to this the relative inability of medical resources to free people of their addictions, I would assert that embracing faith to be a much lesser evil. And certainly less expensive!

Such an observation is backed up by the work of Dr. George Eman Vaillant, a professor of psychiatry at the prestigious Harvard Medical School. Dr. Vaillant is also director of research at the Brigham and Women's Hospital of Boston and the recipient of numerous awards and distinctions. As director for more than thirty years of the long-term Grant Study, he got an up-close look at long-term human behavior. This study followed two groups over a total of sixty-eight years— a group of Harvard students from the years 1939 to 1944 (including President John F. Kennedy), and a group of disadvantaged youths from Boston's inner city. Researchers followed these subjects, all American and white, from youth or young adulthood until they were at least seventy years old.

The research team evaluated participants at least every two years with the help of questionnaires and information from medical treatments regarding their physical and mental health. Researchers also looked at career development, marriage, and (later) retirement. The study's goal was to highlight predictive factors of good aging. The results became the object of two books and an excellent summary published in June of 2009 in *The Atlantic*. Titled "What Makes Us Happy?" the summary highlighted seven factors that facilitate happy aging, both from a physical and psychological point of view:

- A good level of education
- A stable marriage
- Abstaining from tobacco
- Moderate consumption of alcohol
- The regular practice of a physical exercise
- The maintenance of good body weight
- Mature, adaptive mechanisms
  These adaptive mechanisms included altruism, humor, anticipation (foresee coming problems), suppression (the deliberate decision to not jump to conclusions in the face of a problem or conflict in

order to later confront it in an opportune manner) and sublimation (to find distractions from one's emotions, such as channeling aggressiveness into a sport, for example).[1]

The study allowed for the inclusion of other contributors to happiness in adulthood. For example, those tending to be pessimistic appeared to suffer more exposure to disease than optimists. But for Vaillant, social skills—more than intellectual capacity or sociocultural level—seemed to offer the strongest inclination toward happiness at an advanced age. According to the study's data, in one's fifties the ability to establish warm relationships is the best predictor of adapting successfully to older age. Such factors as a healthy life, good adaptive abilities in the face of uncertainty, optimism, and strong relationships certainly don't pose an outright link to spirituality. Yet it is safe to say that all the necessary ingredients for happy aging are produced by a living, active faith life.

Vaillant addressed the issue of faith and spirituality head-on in his 1983 book, *The Natural History of Alcoholism*. For the Harvard psychiatrist, everything negative that critics of religion proffer is like a tree attempting to mask the forest of faith's therapeutic benefits. This addictions specialist confirms that "if they are to recover, powerful new sources of self-esteem and hope must be discovered."[2]

For Professor Vaillant, the healing of addictions is a primary benefit of faith: "Religion provides fresh impetus for both hope and enhanced self-care. Second, if the established alcoholic is to become stably abstinent, enormous personality changes must take place. It is not just coincidence that we associate such dramatic changes with the experience of religious conversion."[3]

Many addicts who make a decision to convert and allow Christ to direct their lives find the reassurance necessary to carry on without their former crutch. In addition, they draw encouragement from members of the community they attend (provided those people are prepared to welcome addicts and don't ostracize them because of their past). Vaillant also speaks of the feelings of forgiveness that play a crucial role in a convert's life, most notably in breaking the vicious cycle of anger and guilt, which increases distress and prompts further drug consumption in hopes of relieving anxiety.

PIETY PROTECTS

Other studies verify Vaillant's research, such as the Piedmont study conducted in North Carolina. Its findings were published in 1994 in the journal, *Hospital & Community Psychiatry*. A survey of three thousand adults, ages eighteen to ninety-seven, sought to test the benefits of faith and worship in preventing the abuse of alcohol. The common feature among the subjects: a history of alcohol addiction, whether recent or prolonged. Researchers posed several questions to evaluate patients' faith and religious practice. In particular they asked about frequency of participation in religious services, personal prayer and Bible reading practices, the importance they placed on religion, and whether they defined themselves as "born again."

The study covered a range of backgrounds and denominational affiliations, from such traditional backgrounds as Orthodox or Reformed, to others, such as Pentecostals. The results were particularly instructive. Recent alcoholism was less common among those with a personal spiritual practice (prayer, Bible reading). Recent and past alcoholism was also less common among those who regularly attend worship services. Persons who went to church at least once a week had a one-third lower risk of alcoholism, compared to those who attended less often. Religion also appeared to cushion the risk of turning to alcohol or helping those mired in to its use to regain sobriety.

Another observation: among those who described themselves as "born again," the proportion of new or old alcoholics was lower than among other groups. In this way the Piedmont study highlighted that whatever the Christian environment to which one belongs, personal piety is of utmost importance to protect against the abuse of alcohol—even more so than the type of church one attends.[4]

However, while alcohol and other illegal toxins are responsible for serious health problems, tobacco remains the most consumed addictive legal substance and is responsible for the greatest mortality rates. Cigarettes kill more than 480,000 people in the United States every year. The ho-hum attitude toward the dangers of cigarettes are the same as treating the equivalent of four Boeing 747s crashing every day with casual indifference!

This situation begs the question of whether religion allows for the protection against the detrimental effects of tobacco. It would seem so, according to "The Relationship Between Religious Activities and Cigarette Smoking in Older Adults," a study published in 1998 in *The Journal of Gerontology*. Conducted at Duke University, the study followed approximately four thousand people living in North Carolina, a heartland for tobacco companies and one where tobacco use is most prevalent in the US. Here again, researchers evaluated the religious activities of participants along with their tobacco consumption. The results speak for themselves:

- The subjects who participated regularly in religious services, or who practiced prayer or Bible reading in private, smoked less.

- The subjects who participated in a service at least once a week and at the same time engaged in prayer and Bible reading had a 90 percent lower risk than those less engaged.

- Those who satisfied themselves with watching televised religious programs were not particularly protected against the risk of nicotine addiction. However, the viewers who smoked and watched these

programs smoked fewer cigarettes than
the other smokers.[5]

Harold Koenig, the principal investigator of this
study, emphasized an interesting fact: "Nearly 60 percent of our sample were Baptist.... They came of age
during the Great Depression and World War II, when
smoking was an inexpensive and popular way to cope
with widespread stress. I found it very interesting that
the lower rates of cigarette smoking among these religious active older people were not due to their having
broken the habit, but rather to their never having
smoked. That demonstrates a remarkable level of resis-
tance to peer pressure for North Carolinians of their
generation."[6]

Still, breaking the smoking habit is a challenge for
many users. While medications exist to help people
stop, long-term abstinence most often poses problems.
Despite this challenge, it appears that spirituality leads
to higher success rates. Believers who develop a personal piety are also those in which the levels of stress
and anxiety are statistically the lowest—a prime asset
in seeking to free oneself from addiction.

FOOD ADDICTIONS

Food is not officially considered as addictive, although
some specialists believe some nutritional behaviors
mimic other addictions. This is especially true of
patients suffering from compulsive eating disorders,
such as anorexia or bulimia, or who experience irre-
pressible desires to eat to calm feelings of anxiety.

Moreover, obese or overweight patients often suffer from a degraded body image and low self-esteem. While numerous alternatives are available for those who wish to lose weight, numerous patients beg non-stop for the miracle diet or magic pill that will make them skinnier with close to no effort. Unfortunately such a pill does not exist! Evidence shows that nearly everyone who loses weight thanks to a diet usually gains back all the weight—or even more. Furthermore, continually attempting a temporary method to effect a permanent change creates the famous yo-yo effect, which little by little makes subsequent attempts less effective.

An approach based in spirituality represents an interesting alternative. First Place for Health is a program created in 1981 in a Baptist church in Houston, Texas. First Place offers a comprehensive approach to the problem, including putting in proper perspective weight loss as part of an individual's overall health. While losing weight is part of the program, and often a primary motivator, it seeks to help people regain control of their body image, restore damaged emotions, and teach them to eat differently and keep moving.

Nothing new, you say? Certainly, but only if you exclude the fact that the program is based on a biblical and spiritual approach. This program places redemption in Christ at the forefront to impact all areas of the participant's life: emotional, mental, spiritual, and physical. It includes weekly small group studies, which include recommendations for dietary planning, physical activities, and everyday spiritual exercises. The latter helps provide relief of the anxiety and tensions that often cause excessive or unhealthy dietary behaviors. With First Place, the only guarantee for success—the long-term engagement necessary for lasting behavioral change—comes from the faith of the participants.

CHAPTER 4

FAITH AND PSYCHOLOGICAL TROUBLES

Be anxious for nothing, but in everything, by prayer and supplication with gratitude, make your requests known to God. And the peace of God, which surpasses all understanding, will protect your hearts and minds through Christ Jesus.

—PHILIPPIANS 4:6-7

A REPORT PUBLISHED IN 2011 showed that America's use of psychotropic medications steadily increased during a recent decade. During the year prior to the release of the report, one in every five adults took at least one psychiatric medication. Among women, it was one in four. The Medco Health Solutions study analyzed trends in mental health medication use among approximately 2.5 million people with health insurance coverage. It compared the use of antidepressants, antipsychotics, attention deficit hyperactivity disorder (ADHD) drugs, and antianxiety treatments from 2001 through 2010.

One can analyze these figures in every manner possible. In an attempt to discredit the findings, critics can point to pressure exerted by the powerful pharmaceutical industry or a lack of training among doctors for too easily prescribing these medications. Yet, the fact is that a high demand for these medications exists, one that reflects a profound discontentment with life and a real suffering of our contemporaries. A realistic picture of the truth is difficult to ignore.

The reasons for consultations with mental health specialists are varied. They range from simple anxiety to panic disorders, and on up the scale to depressive symptoms. But this is only the tip of the iceberg. For the doctor who "digs" a little, numerous physical disorders, such as musculoskeletal disorders (MSD), certain skin problems, digestive disorders, or sleeping disorders, often have roots in chronic stress or anxiety. And conditions are far from improving. Among the negative factors are the disintegration of the family unit, physical isolation, the pressure of a hyper-speed-paced working world, social moroseness, a lack of hope (whether short- or long-term), and a lack of psychological resources. Our patients feel all these factors rushing headlong at them. Not surprisingly, anxiety levels in the modern world are high.

Numerous studies in the mental health field reveal that those who turn to faith and spirituality to deal with twenty-first century pressures enhance their ability to cope. A detailed overview of these results would prove tedious, but it is possible to grasp the most important points that emerge from these surveys, most of them conducted in the United States.

Spiritual practices are positively related to a certain number of indicators of well-being, such as joy of living and satisfaction with life. As mentioned previously, the *Handbook of Religion and Health* lists numerous studies conducted on this subject. Eighty percent of the works report (at the very least) a significant correlation between religious practices and positive indicators of mental health.

The same is true of optimism and a vision of the future, which are determining factors for progressing peacefully through life. In the past, few published studies had shown that patients who rely on faith are more optimistic than other people. Yet hope in the future makes up an integral part of spirituality, which brings the kind of assurance—even in the most somber periods—that the psalmist speaks of: "Even though I walk through the valley of the shadow of death, I will fear no evil, for You are with me" (Ps. 23:4). Thus, even the circumstances that put our lives in peril are not devastating; a person of faith is convinced that this life is only a prelude to a greater existence. Furthermore, the Bible teaches people not to base their hope in life on this earth. For the Christian who puts his or her hope in the mystery of the Resurrection, the present is only a prelude to another dimension. Faith brings a meaning of existence to the believer, a coherency that can only feed hope and optimism: "I fear no evil, for You are with me."

THE MEANING OF EXISTENCE

In the meaning of existence you perhaps have the ingredient that makes for the greatest defect among modern people. In a world where safe havens have vanished, what remains for much of the population? Personal relationships? Family? Work? Political engagements? We live in a society where everything appears to be crumbling, relativism seems to prevail in most realms, and the world is ruled by the ephemeral. No matter how much skeptics scoff, believers find hope in the promise: "Now faith is the substance of things hoped for, the evidence of things not seen" (Heb. 11:1). Assurance, conviction, and hope in the future represent one of the greatest benefits one can derive from faith. Another is the feeling one is not here by accident, which means divine purpose moves the believer forward. So, is it any wonder that the majority of studies show a statistical correlation between the level of faith engagement and the feeling of having a goal in life?

Self-confidence is an indispensable ingredient for a psychologically stable life. Initially one receives such a healthy outlook from one's parents (or, possibly grandparents) and later from people who are dear to you, as well as professional peers. Yet these sources of acknowledgement can also dry up, little by little. Significant influences in our lives die or move away, and changes in the workplace can leave people floundering as they try to adapt.

Quite often the worst self-images of those with psychological struggles originated in childhood. Should you need a reminder, stroll around any park or shopping area on the weekend and listen to annoyed, stressed-out parents reprimand their children. In modern homes television sets often play the role of nanny, with parents either emotionally absent or too overworked to share quality moments with their children. In elementary school, and later in high school, the psychological abuse continues. While many school systems have banned corporal punishment, what about the hurtful verbal remarks and other humiliations children face? Sometimes the damage is inflicted by those who are supposedly there to help the child. When such behavior comes from authority figures and is repeated often enough, it can profoundly impact a person and degrade his or her self-image.

Things don't always look up once we reach adulthood. The professional environment can be the most harmful. In modern life the individual is gradually disappearing from the radar screens of importance. Businesses and other enterprises often view people as mere pawns, there to meet productivity targets and superiors' objectives. Often questionable management techniques exert pressures of all kinds—even moral harassment—without additional compensation for extra duties. There is an ever-present threat of being laid off for failing to meet the pace. It is not surprising that depression and suicide in professional arenas continue to rise. In a recent year more than forty-one thousand Americans killed themselves and nearly five hundred thousand with self-inflicted injuries were treated in emergency departments.[1]

By contrast, a stable Christian environment that teaches moral values, self-respect, and caring for others helps build a healthy self-image. In God's eyes there are no inferior people or outcasts. The Bible teaches that each person has importance in the kingdom of God, and that an intimate relationship with God strengthens the individual. Thousands of years ago, David wrote, "I praise you because I am fearfully and wonderfully made" (Ps. 139:14, NIV).

Of the twenty-nine surveys of this topic, sixteen reported that people who are the most invested spiritually enjoy a positive self-image. By contrast, a study published in 1995 by the University of Michigan's School of Public Health revealed that self-esteem tends to be lower among people with little religious commitment. By teaching people to reject feelings of condemnation, while also avoiding an overly lofty opinion of self, the Bible offers everyone a balanced vision of self that is in harmony with reality.

STRENGTHENING THE SOCIAL FABRIC

In addition, spiritual communities' mutual engagement and sharing of life help strengthen their followers. They allow for the giving and receiving of help and create a stronger social fabric. In modern society an increasing number of people live alone. Consequently many suffer emotional deprivation. A church or parish can allow isolated individuals and those with limited social skills to find a welcoming place (though, unfortunately, not all spiritual communities are receptive to "outsiders.")

Few studies highlight the relationship between spiritual engagement and feelings of solitude. Harold Koenig lists fewer than a dozen in the *Handbook of Religion and Health*. Of these studies, four reveal that feelings of solitude are lower among those who actively practice their religion. Three do not show a link, two yield mitigated results, and one even shows a negative association. These results show that nothing that may appear obvious—such as interaction in a community—should ever be taken for granted. We need to constantly strive to improve hospitality and relationships in our communities, spiritual or otherwise.

In regard to depression, a review of scientific literature reveals that the most spiritually engaged persons are also less subject to depressive disorders. Some 65 percent of the studies in this field show a positive relationship between the degree of religious involvement and a lower frequency of depression. I discovered twenty-two extensive studies in this field that examined people over extended time periods. Sixty-eight percent of these long-term studies demonstrated that the risk of one day of suffering from depressive disorder decreases in proportion to individuals' religious involvement. Moreover, eight clinical essays reviewed the effects of spiritual care on depressive patients.

Five showed that patients receiving spiritual care healed more quickly, in a statistically significant way, in comparison with a control group receiving conventional care.

As for a related field of study, the suicide rate is significantly lower among practicing believers. Fifty-seven of the sixty-eight studies (84 percent) dedicated to the subject showed an inverse relation between religious involvement and resorting to suicide. The large majority of persons questioned in these surveys declared having a negative opinion of suicide. Eleven of these studies examined "assisted suicide," with similar results.

With regards to anxiety, be it a chronic condition or a reaction to a particular situation, the majority of the seventy-six listed studies—including five prospective studies and seven clinical essays—showed that believers engaged spiritually suffered less from psychological disorders than others. This benefit was even observed in studies of patients infected with HIV, or those suffering from obsessive-compulsive disorders. Six of the seven clinical essays showed a benefit particular to spiritual care for these anxiety disorders. In short denying psychologically troubled patients the possibility that religion could help alleviate some of their suffering could be considered malpractice—if not legally then certainly ethically.

CHAPTER 5

MIND GAMES

Come to Me, all you who labor and are heavily
burdened, and I will give you rest. Take My yoke
upon you, and learn from Me. For I am meek and
lowly in heart, and you will find rest for your souls.
For My yoke is easy, and My burden is light.

—MATTHEW 11:28-30

WHILE INFECTIOUS DISEASES continue to be
the principal cause of death in low-income
countries, cardiovascular diseases account for the most
victims globally, regardless of income levels. An average
of 7.3 million people die annually from an ischemic
heart disease, and another 6.2 million from a stroke or
other cerebrovascular disease. In high-income countries cardiovascular and cerebrovascular diseases and
cancer are leading killers, while depression and anxiety
disorders are the principal cause of lost productivity.
These problems occur more frequently in women than

in men. Thus, the illnesses threatening the most people are those provoked by chronic aggression.

The common denominator of these health problems appears to be the response to stress. The publication in 2004 of the INTERHEART study in the renowned journal *The Lancet* established stress as one of the nine universal risk factors driving the occurrence of a myocardial infarction (heart attack). Among these risk factors, stress ranks third, just after high cholesterol and tobacco use. Moreover, the study demonstrated that subjects victim to chronic stress smoke the most (to de-stress?) and have the highest cholesterol levels (compensatory consumption of junk food?), which radically elevates the risk of heart attack. Incidentally among subjects subject to continuing stress twice as many patients were victims of a heart attack than a control group of patients not affected by a cardiovascular condition. This was the first study showing that stress is a factor independent of cardiovascular risk.

We have to appreciate that previously our nervous system had been left largely unchanged for about 160,000 years. Even during the onset of the modern era's Industrial Age, the pressures facing people were far less. It's not that life was once necessarily any easier, but people didn't live with constant stress. Today's stress presents situations for which people don't possess any natural defenses. There is a permanent conflict between our brains as God designed them and the twenty-first-century environment. Modern societies worldwide constantly emit alarming messages that bombard our thoughts. Such input plays on the opposing reflexes of frustration and fear. No matter what the misfortune we cannot run to escape it, organize ourselves in packs, or lay out traps to defend ourselves in the ways our prehistoric ancestors could.

Aside from factors that exceed our capacity to react, many live in a permanent state of stress. Such immersion inflicts recurring damage on the nervous system, immune system, and the rest of the body. Each time that stress manifests itself, we react mentally, physically, and unconsciously. The interaction between the onslaught of messages and our body's capacity to deal with them are comparable to jamming ten pounds of nails into a five-pound sack. This further aggravates our inner feelings about the overload and helps create chronic stress. Such stress holds us in a permanently alert state that restricts our judgment and reactions and often traps us in a web of fear. Mentally we rationalize this overload, shrugging, "It's not that bad." However, this and other rationalizations for our fears don't erase reality. Too much stress renders us incapable of expressing appropriate reactions.

IMPACTING OUR BRAINS

Modern research has shown how what we live through today has the power to permanently affect our brains. Contrary to what scientists thought only a few decades ago, the adult brain does not remain in a fixed state. It is not—as once thought—a finite organ, made up of neurons that fade with age and are never renewed. Recent discoveries have shown that stem cells exist in certain zones of the brain and are capable of rapidly dividing themselves. They also can migrate and tailor themselves to replace other cells. We also know that learning stimulates this division and cellular specialization. In other words, our experiences shape our brain, for the better—or worse!

Today's prevailing concept is that our nervous system was not designed to withstand the level of stress caused by modern life. This results as much from the nature of the stressful events, as it does the ways in which we are equipped to confront them. Modern men and women are confronted by a permanent dilemma. First, people face a fictionalized ideal created by popular culture that says we live in a world where everything is possible. As a result we are supposed to be beautiful, reliable, in good health, and possess everything "fashionable." However, this collides with the reality many of us face. We have a hard time advancing, seem to continually run into doors slamming shut, fail at finding fulfilling relationships, struggle to achieve the ideal image, and cannot afford much.

In an attempt to cope with this conflict, we develop what psychotherapist Richard O'Connor calls "continual stress." The longtime director of the Northwest Center for Family Service and Mental Health in Connecticut is author of several books, including *Undoing Perpetual Stress*. In it O'Connor explains that stress is our organism's normal, passing response in the face of danger or aggression, after which we return to a "basal" state. On the other hand, continual stress is an abnormal response—a bit like a light switch that stays stuck in the "on" position.

"We become caught in a vicious circle," he writes, "in which the effects of stress on our minds damage our bodies and brains in a measurable, physical way; and these physical changes further affect our minds—the way we think, feel and relate—in an invisible, unconscious way. Physical and mental, observable, and unconscious—these injuries reinforce each other, trapping us in a cycle from which there seems to be no escape. We feel the effects of perpetual stress in many different ways: as depression and anxiety; as physical symptoms; as motivations for addictions, as dysfunctional relationships, and as empty and unhappy lives."[1]

A COMPLEX ORGAN

The brain is a system of unbelievable complexity, composed of interconnected structures, themselves made up of specialized neurons that complete certain functions. To communicate between themselves and circulate information, these brain cells use chemical substances, called neurotransmitters or neuromodulators. There are more than fifty varieties of neurons, each exercising a particular action on the cell nucleus and determining which type of signal cell should react.

In childhood these cerebral structures are indistinguishable. It is the developmental process that progressively enables the neural networks to become more sophisticated. All the highly developed functions of an adult genius potentially exist in the brain of a child; in a way they are genetically preprogrammed to develop. However, recent studies have shown that the adult brain continues to develop new circuits and structures throughout life, including the most advanced age. These developments enhance our capacity to accomplish tasks (i.e., play music, memorize a text, or refine one's sense of smell). They also improve our psychological capabilities, such as identifying and modulating our emotions, creating a satisfying self-image, or increasing our empathy. The management of our life experiences thus plays a crucial role in our capacity to be deeply affected, and to be able to elaborate thoughts and our vision of the world.

Our brain is not only the headquarters of our thoughts and reactions, it is also involved in the body's management. It is at the center of the nervous system that allows for regulation of such automatic functions as digestion, breathing, arterial circulation, blood pressure, and secretion and excretion of fluids. The regulating centers of the autonomous nervous system are situated in the spinal cord, the brain, and the brain stem (a zone located between the brain and spinal cord).

This autonomous nervous system directs two distinct systems. There is the parasympathetic nervous system, which contributes to organs' slowing down and stimulation of the digestive system. The other is the sympathetic nervous system, which enables the body to respond to emergencies and prepare physical and intellectual activity (expansion of the bronchial tubes, acceleration of cardiac and respiratory activity, or dilation of the pupils). These two systems exert diametrically-opposed actions on the same organ. When one stimulates a function, the other stifles it.

The nervous impulses coming from the autonomous nervous system do not take a direct action on the organ in question. The orders reach the organ through chemical mediators that are released at the nerve endings: the neurotransmitters. The reaction of stress causes the intervention of two major categories of chemical mediators:

- Catecholamines

  These are freed by the adrenal medulla (adrenaline) and the neuron terminals of the sympathetic autonomic nervous system. Catecholamines are responsible for the majority of the instant responses to aggression: acceleration of the heart rate, increase in blood pressure, redistribution of the viscera's blood toward the muscles and brain, increase of pupil diameter, bronchial dilation, or hyperglycemia.

- Glucocorticoids

  The glucocorticoids come to relieve and amplify the action of the catecholamines—mainly on an energetic level—by encouraging sugar production from non-glucidic sources.

CREATING STRESS

The difficulties that assail the body in its day-to-day functioning are not of the same nature as those used by researchers to study the biology of stress. Medical practitioners speak of life events to point out either everyday situations or those that occur occasionally and require adaptation by an individual. Stress can mean everything that damages the body's equilibrium, including the anticipation of an unpleasant event. Our capacity to think and imagine allow us— rightly or wrongly—to think up a harmful situation and touch off a stress response as powerful as the one caused by the situation itself! Response to stress can arise simply because one *fears* it might happen. In an age of terrorism, cataclysmic natural disasters, and instantaneous worldwide communication, modern society offers multiple occasions for dread of what tomorrow may bring.

This demonstrates how stress involves more than our life experiences; it also originates with a person's perceptions, including mental representations and behavior. Thus, it is not only the characteristics of the aggressive situation that are important, but also the possibility of the individual modifying it through behavior. Even then, behavioral control is not the only factor at play. There is what we call "predictive capacity." In other words, the individual's expectations of how a situation will develop over time and the consequences his or her actions will play on the outcome.

In the face of a stressful situation the possibility to control the situation and to predict the outcome plays a key role in an individual's outlook. We call this "adjustment strategies." The possibility to confront a situation effectively lies not only in someone's ability to select an appropriate strategy. It also involves his or her ability to utilize available social resources. Generally speaking, physiological stress induced by an aggressive situation weakens when the subject has foresight and behavioral control. There are also benefits from a positive attitude from peers and family.

A sector of research has seen an important development over the course of the past decade: neuropsychoimmunology, or the study of the relationship between the brain and the immune system. Numerous studies carried out on laboratory animals exposed to various stress factors show that their immune responses are quite sensitive to aggression. As an example, the exposure to inevitable or unpredictable electric shocks in a rat diminished the capacity of white blood cells involved in the immune reaction to replicate themselves. These electric shocks do not have an effect when they are controllable or foreseeable. Scientists have observed the same phenomena in humans exposed to such unexpected events as grief, a parent's disease, conjugal difficulties, or competition.

In the past doctors tended to explain the effects of stress on immunity by the suppressive power of glucocorticoids, which are chemicals that fight inflammation in the body. However, we now know that the mechanisms at play are much more complex. There is a network of reciprocal interactions between the nervous system and the immune system. The primary lymphoid organs (the thymus) and the secondary (the spleen, the ganglions) are supplied with nerves by the sympathetic branch of the autonomic nervous system. The nerve fibers accompany the blood vessels, and then divide themselves to wait for the zones of maturation and storage of the lymphocytes, or the organisms' main defense cells.

This means that the composition of the microenvironment in which the lymphocytes are immersed depends on the level of sympathetic activity. The immune cells possess receptors on the surface membranes that allow for the fixation of the majority of neurotransmitters. These receptors have biochemical characteristics similar to those of the receptors situated on the neurons. Thus, they provide the immune cells with a veritable reader system for the nervous system's operation. Due to close ties between the nervous system and the immune system, stress can affect the immune defense reactions through multiple channels. This ranges from the activation of the sympathetic nervous system to the release of glucocorticoids.

Looking at the Whole Person

I know this discussion has been a bit technical, but to simplify: when you are confronted with any event, your brain will first analyze the situation to determine its nature. If the surroundings become too elevated for a simple adjustment to allow for a normal response, it will trigger a behavior. For that to occur, a new program must go into play. Up to this point organic reactions assure maintenance of the body's internal environment. Now they are required to ensure the autonomy required for a "fight or flight" response. Thus, the body will no longer preserve stability; on the contrary, it will abandon it! Only then will a return to internal homeostasis become possible.

For example, following a shock that results in trauma during a fight, the individual will "forget" the associated pain, and the brain will determine whether to continue fighting or flee the danger. The tissular repair will stop and be deferred until later (until after the fight or the person runs out of harm's way). It will only take hold again when the subject is calm and relaxed. This dynamic itself depends on all of the person's previous neuroendocrinal-metabolic history—that is to say, the historic relationships with these environments and the circumstances faced in the past.

Contrary to what has long been taught in Western medical facilities, today we know that the human organism makes up an indissoluble whole. This whole interacts with its environment through the central and peripheral nervous systems. The mental and emotional states in which we find ourselves exert a direct influence on the operation of our organs through our autonomic nervous system and immune system. Yet, it is still quite challenging in the West to depart from an exclusively organic and symptomatic approach to medicine. This ignores the overall dimension of patients, most notably their mind-body relationships.

In recent years in the United States the most prestigious universities have examined the relationship between the body and the mind. In such environments students review—in the most scientific manner possible—the influence of spirituality on health and longevity, the impact of positive psychology, and the effects of religious practice and prayer for the sick. It is a dramatically different approach that has borne considerable fruit. For one, these studies show the devastating impact the pace of modern life makes on our health. They also demonstrate the benefits one can expect from spiritual practices, both preventive and healing. A fancy word *neuropsychoimmunology* constitutes an essential part of this new approach. This discipline is now known as a distinct theme at international medical conferences and is the subject of high-level scholarly reviews.

Some of this understanding originated with work from decades ago. In 1981 Robert Ader, David M. Felten, and Nicholas Cohen released the first edition of their book, *Psychoneuroimmunology*. This eponymous reference work, now in its fourth edition (the various works have ranged from seventeen chapters to a few volumes), allowed for the regrouping of a body of diverse works under the same appellation. It has helped the medical community better understand the interactions between the brain and the immune system on one hand, and performance and health on the other.

For three decades researchers have been trying to identify the multiplicity of familial and social factors that contribute to illnesses. For example, studies have reviewed the types of people who are prone to suffer from peptic ulcers, heart attacks, autoimmune diseases, and cancers. Conversely others are looking at the impact of strong coping skills on healing. In their 2002 book, *The Link Between Religion and Health: Psychoneuroimmunology and the Faith Factor*, Harold Koenig and Jay Cohen reviewed the studies in fields as varied as cancer, susceptibility to infections, wound healing, and autoimmune diseases.

STRENGTH IN SOCIAL SUPPORT

In the case of cancer researchers discovered that religious beliefs and practices allow patients to find meaning in their existence despite this hardship. Furthermore, the communal life they enjoy offers social support. This allows for the patient to find understanding and encouragement in the fight against the disease, and experience lowered stress and anxiety. An increasing number of studies reveal the advantageous role psychosocial factors—including spiritual life—offer against this formidable class of diseases.

With regards to infections, stressful situations have been shown to be associated with a lowering of immune defenses, which promotes susceptibility to infections. Considerable research has shown how social factors, such as a network of acquaintances and friends, positively influences immune cellular (activation and mobilization of "killer" cells) and humoral (production of antibodies) responses. Doctors have also learned that positive social factors protect against the triggering of infectious pathologies such as the flu or herpes, and accelerates bodily healing.

More surprising are studies of tissue healing. As I explained earlier, psychological stress leads to the activation of the sympathetic autonomous nervous system. This leads to a narrowing of the arteries and a reduction in blood supply to peripheral parts of the body in order to supply more food and oxygen to vital organs such as the heart, kidneys, and brain. However, if this situation persists, the lack of the oxygen supply at the peripheral level (skin and organ casing) can lead to damage.

To take a closer look at the subject of stress and healing, noted behavioral medicine researcher Janice Kiecolt-Glaser set out to compare the rates of healing between individuals who faced serious stress and those who didn't. A professor at the Ohio State University College of Medicine, Kiecolt-Glaser conducted a skin biopsy on thirteen patients, all suffering from Alzheimer's and thus subjected to constant stress. She carried out the same biopsies in thirteen non-stressed patients. She discovered the time of healing for those who were under stress increased by 24 percent. Among humans and animals, these results have been confirmed by other similar findings; all showed stress led to a slower rate of healing.[2]

Another study examined dental surgery students who had had biopsies taken inside their mouths. The first came during the relaxed summer months. Researchers took the second on the opposite side of the mouth three days before finals. Each student had two identical wounds in the mouth. The first took an average of eight days to heal. That compared to an average of eleven days for healing of the second wound, taken during a much more stressful period. That is nearly a 40 percent difference. It is interesting to note that once the exams passed, the level of stress decreased considerably, but the wounds' tissular healing was still delayed. This is logical, since tissular healing responds to a complicated stream of biological events. If the initial steps are disrupted by stress, the whole stream is modified, which slows healing.[3]

THE VALUE OF SPIRITUALITY

To my knowledge no specific studies have shown that religious practice allows for the acceleration of healing of wounds. Still, there is evidence this is the case. First, it is understood that well-developed spirituality lowers stress levels. In addition, several studies have shown that religious activities improve patients' post-operational state. This includes a reduction in complications, more rapid recovery, and lower consumption of pain relievers among patients receiving regular visits from chaplains and benefiting from the encouragements of their faith community.

In the aforementioned *The Link Between Religion and Health* Koenig and Cohen dedicated an entire chapter to studies of patients infected with HIV. Some demonstrated that a certain number of psychosocial factors are statistically associated with disturbances of the immune system, thus risking a faster progression of the disease.

The authors identified several factors that prompted the disease to progress. Among them were life's afflictions, such as grief, chronic stress, or pessimism; and the absence of social cohesion. Conversely a certain number of studies carried out in patients infected with HIV showed that religion and spirituality played a positive role in the way these patients managed their disease. Faith allowed them to better confront their personal difficulties and restored hope and optimism. This helped them relax, combat fear and anxiety, and successfully lean on a social network for moral support.

Spiritual support extends to helping people deal with mental conflict amid physical disabilities and diseases. Koenig and Cohen's studies showed how the hostility and anger that stem from various conditions and disease can damage one's health. The negative repercussions include an increased likelihood of disease and mortality. Aggressiveness modifies behavior and lifestyle, leading to more accidents and increased consumption of alcohol, tobacco, and drugs. Hostile or aggressive behavior is also associated with a series of physical problems, ranging from heart troubles to lowered immunity.

Different surveys show that aggressive or angry personalities tend to be egocentric and ready to express negative opinions of others. As long ago as the 1970s cardiologists Meyer Friedman and Ray Roseman highlighted the character traits common to those with a higher risk of heart attack. The two personality types are widely known as type A and type B. Type A personalities are generally impatient, aggressive, and unable to relax. In general these subjects have a tendency toward irritability and a latent hostility yearning for expression. By contrast, type B personalities are known for their patience, optimism, tolerance, attentiveness to others, and an ability to let go of irritations.

While many have documented the risks of type A behaviors, fewer have highlighted the benefits of type B behaviors. Among those who have is Berton Kaplan, an epidemiologist at the University of North Carolina. In a 1992 article in *The Journal of Behavioral Medicine* titled "Social Health and the Forgiving Heart: The Type B Story," he wrote that there are four cardinal virtues linked to type B behavior: self-esteem, the ability to forgive, sociability, and a certain wisdom when it comes to the reasons behind certain events.[4] These virtues all offer health benefits and a well-lived spiritualty will help develop them.

I can't overstate the value of the spiritual life when considering the plethora of studies in human psychology and pathophysiology that illustrate how human beings are not "designed" to withstand too much adversity. Some are clear; for example, humans cannot survive the absence of oxygen—which is indispensable to life—for long. Nor can they withstand lack of sleep. An utter loss of sunlight, prolonged physical inactivity, or a massive absorption of calories will manifest themselves and cause serious diseases. Thanks to clinical and epidemiological studies we know that certain mental states and beliefs can also damage our health.

Thankfully recent years have seen a conjoining of scientific conclusions and spiritual precepts developed in the Bible (particularly the New Testament). In this way the numerous teachings of Jesus and the apostles are not simply rigid moral dictates. They also represent inspired instructions that will help protect our lives. The health benefits available by following the Scripture's teachings invite us to review with a new eye. By implementing them, we can enjoy better health—both mentally and physically.

CHAPTER 6

THE SHIELD OF FAITH

In every situation take the shield of faith,
and with it you will be able to extinguish
all the flaming arrows of the evil one.

—EPHESIANS 6:16, HCSB

B EYOND THE RESEARCH showing that religious
practice and faith can reduce the impact of
psychological disorders, it is interesting to try to understand and consider why—and how—this positive influence is applied.

In 2007 Wai-keung Yeung, a social sciences
researcher, and Yuk-chung Chan, an associate professor
at the department of applied social sciences of the Hong
Kong Polytechnic University, published an article in the
International Journal of Psychosocial Rehabilitation
titled, "The Positive Effects of Religiousness on Mental
Health in Physically Vulnerable Populations: A Review
on Recent Empirical Studies and Related Theories." This

work synthesized the most recently published studies. It highlighted the benefits of spirituality among those weakened by handicap, disease, or old age. A chart that accompanied it symbolizes the cognitive, spiritual, social, and psychological resources that promote mental health.[1] Each resource exercises beneficial influence while interacting with the others to create a synergistic effect. The spiritual resources from particular faith and religious practice include such elements as hope, the meaning of existence bestowed through the disciple's sense of mission, the hope of eternal life, and reassurance of the love of an all-powerful God. This is enough to transform an individual by freeing him or her from a nihilistic view of one's existence as competitive and purposeless.

Considering one's earthly life from this kind of optimistic view can form a positive cognitive resource that helps an individual to avoid psychological "decomposition" during times of adversity. A positive vision of the world allows for optimists to see the good side of life, and to find the day-to-day desirable and beautiful. In this way, when a painful event occurs, faith allows for the believer to hope for help on behalf of a God he or she considers positively inclined toward His children. The Psalms beautifully express the believer's expectation in adversity: "From where does my help come? My help comes from the LORD, who made heaven and earth. He will not let your foot slip; He who keeps you will not slumber. Behold, He who guards Israel shall neither slumber nor sleep" (Ps. 121:1–4).

Endurance Amid Trouble

Believers who develop an intrinsic spirituality find God's help, grace, and love sufficient. This enables them to keep going, even in life's most somber moments. Indeed, it is often during tragedy and loss that people speak of God. In brief, it results in an assurance that what God has said, He will surely do. Furthermore, sociological researchers have discovered that the most optimistic people enjoy a well-developed social network. Patients find immense benefits from a support group when facing serious medical issues; it provides a kind of psychological cushion to deal with the crisis.

These helpers offer reinforcement for the patient's faith and self-confidence through their presence, prayer, material aid, and other support. Though some term this "intangible," in reality it represents very tangible and valuable assistance. It creates a "virtuous circle" that bolsters the patient's spirit and outlook, strengthens his or her faith, and serves as a buffer against stress. Patients who benefit from such networks are typically supportive of this community's values, traditions, and teachings. In turn (hopefully) this will—in a manner of speaking—put wind in their sails and strengthen their confidence in God.

This circle offers other benefits. For example, by engaging in a community and gradually adopting its values and beliefs, individuals can increase their spiritual resources. These can be such qualities as the notion of the meaning of existence, God's grace, the deliverance offered by an all-powerful God, and the promise of life after death. In addition, it expands the person's circle of friends and acquaintances. These interpersonal relationships and shared beliefs can bolster the individual's psychological and cognitive resources.

Studies have shown that such a network allows for a strong socialization. This enables the individual to gradually grow more confident and optimistic. Instead of seeing the world as a place where "people are out to get me" or where the latest calamity is only moments away, believers are able to see the surrounding society with new eyes. They consider their existence to be a source of joy, which—when they surface—allows a believer to put stressful situations in their proper perspective.[2]

Dr. James Jones, a professor of psychology of religion at Rutgers State University in New Jersey, suggests that spirituality improves an individual's psychological and physical parameters. His article, published in 2004 in the *Journal of Religion and Health*, was titled "Religion, Health and the Psychology of Religion." Among the factors Jones cited were an increase in the relaxation response, a state of deep rest first described by Harvard medical professor Herbert Benson. Jones also listed a decrease in behaviors harmful to one's health, better social support, better adherence to treatments prescribed by doctors, a sense of coherency in existence, a better self-image—which improves self-esteem and reduces anxiety—and a positive synergy between mental and physical well-being. The latter mutually strengthen each other. However, Jones wrote that the benefits of religion do not limit themselves to the beneficial effects of these mediators. He believes that spirituality contributes to humans' well-being in a special and unique manner—beyond the relatively classic factors.[3]

SIGNIFICANT ADVANTAGE

Dr. Jones's view echoes numerous recent studies showing that—after statistically neutralizing the benefit of these factors (for example, comparing Christians to nonreligious subjects who also possessed them)—religion still offers a significant advantage. He concluded that beneficial effects conducive to spirituality must exist, extending beyond classic factors of well-being also identified among nonreligious individuals.

The beneficial effects of religion could be conveyed by a transcendent approach toward life, communicated uniquely through spiritualty. For example, take the particular perspective Christians bring to the meaning of life and death and hope in an afterlife. The author of the epistle to the Hebrews explains how a relationship with Christ can free us from the incertitude common among humans. This outlook can have profound psychological repercussions: "So then, as the children share in flesh and blood, He [Christ] likewise took part in these, so that through death *He might destroy him who has the power of death*, that is, the devil, and deliver those who through fear of death were throughout their lives subject to bondage" (Heb. 2:14–15, emphasis added).

Religious or not, suffering is shared by all humans. However, where the nonbeliever only sees the absurdity of life, sadness, and destruction, people of faith find meaning. The biblical text warns that sufferings common to humans will not spare the believer. Still, in the midst of torment or trouble, persons of faith can find peace and consolation in their relationship with God. As David wrote in the Psalms: "Many are the afflictions of the righteous, but the LORD delivers him out of them all. He keeps all his bones; not one of them is broken.... The LORD redeems the life of his servants; none of those who take refuge in him will be condemned" (Ps. 34:19–20, 22, ESV).

The majority of religions teach that suffering is inevitable, sometimes useful, and possible to overcome. To find meaning in adversity when it reaches us, and to find recourse to confront it with our faith, gives one the strength to pull through. It could also be that practices conducive to spirituality and religion, such as prayer, meditation, or singing, activate particular areas in our brain. This can provide benefits in terms of mental well-being and physical health.

These effects help explain why some religious adherents, even when confronting difficult and challenging situations, uphold a strong psychological balance. I am inevitably reminded of Christians in underdeveloped regions of the world today who are persecuted for their faith (something I have personally witnessed) and yet keep such an appetite and joy for living that millions of people in highly developed societies would envy them!

Whatever the explanations and however passionate they may be, the fact remains—be spiritual and you will feel better and live longer!

CHAPTER 7

WIRED FOR GOD!

For what may be known about God is clear
to them [mankind] since God has shown it
to them. The invisible things about Him—His
eternal power and deity—have been clearly
seen since the creation of the world and are
understood by the things that are made.

—ROMANS 1:19-20

I N RECENT TIMES neuroscientists have investigated the functioning of the brain during prayer, meditation, and states of mystical ecstasy. What emerges from these studies, conducted by neuroimagery—think of the familiar MRI—are pictures of the human brain that help measure spiritual realities. Researchers have discovered that such practices as prayer or meditation improve brain functions and "plasticity," meaning the brain's ability to reorganize its neural pathways. Studies of mystics show unique functioning during spiritual experiences, which cannot be recreated or reproduced by any other technique. So while our brain does not create God, it seems He has conceived this organ as one way of communicating with Him.

A BRAIN FOR GOD

Numerous scientific studies across the world have demonstrated the relationship between personal spirituality and good health, and longer life span. This begs the questions: How can we understand such phenomena? Are they uniquely supernatural? Or do physiological mechanisms exist that help explain them—at least partially?

Above all we must remain humble as we recognize the answers may exceed human reasoning. We cannot unlock the mysteries of faith and transcendence overnight. Still, certain avenues are taking shape. The advancement of knowledge on human physiology, the decrypting of immune system (the guardian of bodily integrity) operations, and the fine-tuning of high-tech imaging tools allow scientists to glean a more comprehensive view of the brain. This enhances our understanding of how faith can influence our physical— particularly our cerebral—functioning.

Some faith practitioners will undoubtedly cry, "Sacrilege." After all, is it legitimate for a believer to see through what appeared previously a matter of mystery? Or miracle? Isn't there the temptation to remove God from the equation and rationalize everything? This is not a new debate. Every science student knows what came of Copernicus and Galileo's calling into question geocentrism—the misguided theory that everything in the solar system revolved around the earth. At the time some priests said these scientists posed an unthinkable challenge to sound biblical doctrine. Copernicus and Galileo correctly saw the sun at the center of our universe. Still, the subsequent, increased depth of knowledge about the universe and matter, and advances in quantum physics, did not render faith obsolete. The advancement of scientific knowledge in no way diminishes the impact of the biblical message, nor the reality of people experiencing God's intervention in their lives.

THE ESSENCE OF MAN

God is a spirit, while man is both spirit and flesh who functions according to biological principles. Because God influences this functioning, human beings intrinsically possess everything necessary to interact with their Creator. Furthermore, those qualities the Gospels present as virtuous seem best adapted to human physiology. Since it is highly unlikely the writers of the Holy Scriptures knew much about the complexity of the mechanisms regulating our organisms, could this have been the fruit of divine inspiration?

God's gateway to the universe appears to be located between our two ears. Our brain sets humans apart from the rest of the animal kingdom. Men and women are the only living beings endowed with the gift of abstract thought and the capability of reflecting on self to create astonishing devices, machines, writings, paintings, music, and other objects that serve to satisfy an appetite for beauty. Early in history, before the appearance of religion, we know that humans erected a sepulcher (admittedly primitive) to honor deceased loved ones. This appears to be the proof that, ever since prehistoric times, humans have wondered about life after this world. No other animal displays such concern.

According to researchers the genomes of man and chimpanzee differ by only 1 percent. Pierre Darlu, a geneticist of evolution, wrote: "The genetic divide between man and chimpanzee is much less than that which separates the two species of orangutan."[1] Yet, those few genes make all the difference. They enable humans to say "I" and bestow them with an insatiable curiosity that incessantly pushes them to stretch the limits of their knowledge and creativity. It also provides humans the capacity to wonder about the future. As Solomon wrote: "I have seen the task that God has given people to keep them occupied. He has made everything appropriate in its time. *He has also put eternity in their hearts*, but man cannot discover the work God has done from beginning to end" (Eccles. 3:10–11, HCSB, emphasis added).

Thus, reason appears to be the sole province of humans. This capacity, which comes from our brain, influences everything about us. Even more so, the quality of this reason is crucial to our functioning; it can safeguard it or destroy it. It is what humans have discerned since ancient times and what modern science is gradually demonstrating.

Pursuing Goals

The director of research at Philadelphia's Thomas Jefferson University Hospital and Medical College, Professor Andrew Newberg is a world-renowned specialist. His specialty is researching the interaction between spirituality and the brain. He was the first scientist to place religious persons (during meditation) inside a magnetic resonance imaging (MRI) machine to observe the inner workings of their brain.

Newberg, the author of such evocatively titled works as *How God Changes Your Brain*, and *Principles of Neurotheology*, explains how the study of the connections between neuroscience and religion allow for the pursuit of four goals:

1. Increase our understanding of the brain and the human mind

2. Help us better understand theology and religion

3. Improve the human condition in the fields of health, quality of life

4. Improve the human condition in the fields of religion and spirituality

Thus, research in this field helped develop methods for objectively measuring the interaction between spirituality and the human brain. For example, during meditation or prayer it is possible to measure the variations of cellular metabolism, concentrations in neurotransmitters, or blood flow in different cerebral zones. Scientists have also measured—again, during religious practices—the autonomous nervous system's activity, which regulates the automatic functioning of our organs. Some spiritual practices modify blood pressure and heart rate. Certain meditative states can be characterized by a sensation of profound calm while still associated with an intense state of mental alertness.

More recently the hormonal and immune function's measurements have enriched the arsenal for further scientific evaluation of religious behaviors. This is of utmost importance, since doctors know that some cancers originate with hormonal or immune dysfunctions. Since cerebral activity is capable of modifying the operation of the endocrine glands and immune system, it can affect this class of diseases.

However, the most spectacular assessment tools for mental states in relation to spirituality are "space age" functional cerebral imaging techniques. The functional MRI, PET scan, or SPECT allow doctors to visualize changes in the brain in response to certain medicines. Depending on the particular technique, it is possible to quantify cerebral blood flow and the concentrations in neurotransmitters such as serotonin, acetylcholine, or dopamine. These may significantly vary in certain zones of the brain during spiritual practices.

PERCEIVING SPIRITUAL DIMENSIONS

These different methods can be utilized to objectify what occurs in the brain when an individual prays, meditates, or has a spiritual experience. In certain cases they also allow one to differentiate what falls in the category of pathological, since certain mental illnesses or drugs can lead to pseudo-spiritual experiences.

"The human brain is conceived in a unique way to perceive and generate spiritual realities," Newberg and Waldman said in *How God Changes Your Brain.* "It uses logic, reason, intuition, imagination, and emotion to integrate God and the universe into a complex system of personal values, behaviors, and beliefs. Neurosciences will never be able to demonstrate to you that God exists or not, but the fact remains that each human brain, since childhood, appears designed to accept the possibility that a spiritual dimension exists. Recently, there has been a spate of antireligious books that argue that religious beliefs are personally and societally dangerous. But the research strongly suggest otherwise.... Our research has led us to the following conclusions:

- "Each part of the brain constructs a different perception of God.

- Every human brain assembles its perceptions of God in uniquely different ways, thus giving God different qualities of meaning and value.

- Spiritual practices, even when stripped of religious beliefs, enhance the neural functioning of the brain in ways that improve physical and emotional health.

- Intense, long-term, contemplation of God and other spiritual values appears to permanently change the structure of those parts of the brain that control our moods, give rise to our conscious notions of self, and shape our sensory perception of the world.

- Contemplative practices strengthen a specific neurological circuit that generates peacefulness, social awareness, and compassion for others."[2]

In addition to these five major areas spiritual practices have proven their effectiveness for improving cognitive functions as a whole, as well as communication and creativity. They may even be capable of modifying our perceptions of reality.

It is worth noting that atheists' reproaches of spiritual practices as detrimental to mental stability do not stem from a scientific view. It is not religion or spirituality per se that is detrimental, but their abuse and misuse. It is especially harmful when it involves zealots who seek to impose on others—in an aggressive or authoritarian manner—their system of beliefs and values.

Fortunately most humans' reasoning capacity allows them to avoid such dictatorial types—and avoid overreacting to them. While people possess a biological and neurological propensity to behave in a hostile or aggressive way, research shows that regular spiritual practices diminish the brain's capacity to respond with anger or fear. To immerse ourselves in contemplation of God modifies the brain in a unique, profound way. Spiritual contemplation strengthens a neuronal circuit that controls sociability and empathy, while inhibiting negative and destructive emotions. For Newberg, it's the type of change we should all strive for, particularly in hopes of reducing the world's proliferating aggressiveness and conflict.

STRENGTHEN YOUR CINGULATE GYRUS!

The discovery of neuroplasticity—the brain's capacity to permanently modify its neuronal connections and functionalities—is the major revolution of recent decades. When we reflect deeply on an entity as complex and mysterious as God, we trigger veritable storms of neuronal activity throughout our brain. New connections appear and others come undone as our thoughts give rise to new perspectives or concepts. The higher the magnitude of the questions, the more our brain develops. Contemplative practices allow us to strengthen our positive perceptions and to become more attentive and compassionate to others.

Compassion appears to depend on a particular cerebral structure known as the anterior cingulate gyrus. This mouthful of a name refers to a small fold in our cerebral cortex, located in front and in the middle of our brain, between the frontal lobe (which regulates our thoughts and behaviors) and the limbic system (which manages our emotions). This maintains a delicate balance. The more the gyrus is developed, the more capable we are of manifesting empathy, and the less susceptible to reacting with fear or anger. If our gyrus is dysfunctional it diminishes our communication skills, and we become incapable of being in synch with what others think or feel. As the studies in functional cerebral imaging have demonstrated, this unique cerebral structure is stimulated during meditation. Thus, the more we develop meditative and spiritual practices, the less inclined we are to act hostile and greedy.

When it comes to our emotions, anger seems the most basic and difficult to control. It puts us on the defensive and creates anxiety and aggression toward others. Anger inhibits the functioning of our frontal lobes. When this happens, we lose all rationality, including an awareness of our actions. When the frontal lobes are inhibited, it becomes impossible to listen to others, or feel the slightest empathy or compassion for them. In such a state the dominant feeling becomes a rigid certainty in our opinions, which interrupts communication. In addition, anger releases a cascade of chemical molecules that inhibit the cerebral zones that control emotions.

To control anger and aggression and respond in an opposite way requires extended practice. Yet, this is the instruction Jesus gave to His disciples: "I say to you, love your enemies, bless those who curse you, do good to those who hate you, and pray for those who spitefully use you and persecute you." (Matt. 5:44). Ever read this verse? The idea that your anterior cingulate gyrus played such a crucial role in implementing Christ's instruction likely never occurred to you. Yet this is what can prevent us from returning evil with evil. If we want to operate in the image of God, we need to be "merciful and gracious, slow to anger, and abounding in mercy" (Ps. 103:8). In other words, we need a fully operational anterior cingulate gyrus!

By focusing consistently on spiritual values and goals, we increase the blood flow in the frontal lobes. This leads to a reduction of the activity of the cerebral centers devoted to emotions. The more we concentrate on developing our spiritual life, the better we can control ourselves. Meditation is one of the means through which we can achieve this goal. Newberg's functional cerebral studies of individuals practicing meditation demonstrated this. The activation of the anterior cingulate gyrus and the prefrontal cortex improves memory and cognitive functions. This counteracts the effects of depression, a frequent consequence of cerebral aging. Therefore, it is supposed that meditative practices help to relieve the effects of these pathologies. An article published in 2007 in the journal *Neurology Today* showed that spiritual practices make it possible to slow the decline of cognitive functions in patients suffering from Alzheimer's disease.[3]

THE KEY TO HAPPINESS?

What happens in our brain when we give ourselves over to meditation? This exercise involves the implementation of several cerebral structures. When we meditate, we focus and benefit from being alert, which increases the activity of our prefrontal cortex. We also increase our empathy and sociability, and exercise control over our movements and emotions.

This affects our sensory perceptions of the world. This combination thus blends concentration with detection of errors, empathy, compassion, and emotional balance, which helps inhibit fear and anger. These functions deteriorate with aging, which contributes to the development of psychological pathologies, such as anxiodepressive disorders or obsessive-compulsive disorders. But regular meditation allows us to preserve and even improve the functionalities of this circuit and prevent disorders linked to its deterioration.

Newberg's studies also showed a notable reduction of activity in the parietal lobes during meditation. This part of the cortex enables us to construct a sense of self. This explains why self-consciousness eventually fades among practitioners of extended meditation. Although we have yet to identify all the factors involved, this loss of self-focus appears to increase the individual's ability to look toward specific goals and to accomplish diverse tasks with increased pleasure.

When this happens, one enters what Mihály Csíkszentmihályi calls the "state of flow," or "optimal experience." This Hungarian psychologist and professor at California's Claremont University has taught at two other academic institutions. Starting in the 1970s, Csíkszentmihályi sought to identify conditions that could characterize the moments people described as "among the best" of their lives. He questioned mountaineers, chess players, music composers, and others who devoted considerable time and energy to activities for the simple pleasure of doing them, without pursuit of conventional gratifications, such as money or social recognition. This research allowed him to define the concept of "flow."

Csíkszentmihályi presented his theory in his seminal work, *Flow: The Psychology of Optimal Experience*. He talked about how individuals are happiest in this state of complete absorption in an activity: "This is what we mean by Optimal Experience. It is what the sailor holding a tight course feels when the winds whips through her hair, when the boat lunges through the waves like a colt—sails, hull, wind, and sea humming a harmony that vibrates in the sailor's veins. It is what a painter feels when the colors on the canvas begin to set up a magnetic tension with each other, and a new thing, a living form, takes shape in front of the astonished creator. Or it is the feeling a father has when his child for the first time responds to his smile. Such events do not occur only when the external conditions are favorable, however: people who have survived concentration camps or who have lived through near-fatal physical dangers often recall that in the midst of their ordeal they experienced extraordinary rich epiphanies in response to such simple events as hearing the song of a bird in the forest, completing a hard task, or sharing a crust of bread with a friend. Contrary to what we usually believe, moments like these, the best moments in our lives, are not the passive, receptive, relaxing times....The best moments usually occur when a person's body or mind is stretched to its limits in a voluntary effort to accomplish something difficult and worthwhile."[4]

Such feelings of freedom, joy, and accomplishment—when time seems to disappear—is something each person can experience. It is a blissful state, one where action and consciousness merge. These phases of optimal performance constitute a source of personal progression as they propel us toward our objectives. In triggering these states, meditation is thus a preferential activity, allowing for the experience of pleasure while advancing toward our goals. According to Newberg, it only takes a few weeks of regularly practicing these exercises to transform the brain's overall operations, a rather remarkable finding.[5]

This demonstrates the extraordinary ability to voluntarily change and improve our neurological functioning. This can literally heal our brain. And, in particular, in zones specific to humans—the frontal lobes (the "headquarters" of creative ability), our aptitudes to reason and communicate, our ability to be at peace with others, and our inclinations toward compassion and motivation.

MEDITATIVE PRACTICE

The Bible contains approximately twenty references to meditative practice, which indicates how this exercise makes up an integral part of a relationship with God. For example, the psalmist declares, "Blessed is the man who walks not in the counsel of the ungodly, but his delight is in the law of the Lord, and in His law he meditates day and night" (Ps. 1:1–2). Elsewhere he says, "My soul will be satisfied as with marrow and fatness, and my mouth will praise You with joyful lips. When I remember You on my bed, and meditate on You in the night watches..." (Ps. 63:5–6). In light of recent discoveries in neurotheology, it is not surprising the Psalms frequently mention meditation as a source of bliss.

Practiced on a daily basis, meditation increases our ability to focus on goals. The frontal lobes—the principal beneficiaries of meditation—indeed compose the spot in our brain where dreams can become a reality. Selective attention is the key to achieving them by giving us the ability to selectively process the plethora of information that bombards us daily. In this way daily meditation increases our ability to focus. Selective attention improves the cerebral circuits devoted to memory, which is indispensable to making good decisions.

Again the Bible offers a telling illustration of this physiological principle. The story appears in Joshua, as Moses's successor prepares to lead Israel into the Promised Land. God addresses Joshua, reminding him what is expected of him. Joshua thus finds himself facing an enormous challenge that surpasses his ability. Several times God tells him to (in effect) strengthen himself. (See Joshua 1:6–7, 9, 18.) In reading Joshua 1, I often wondered what it means to "strengthen yourself," although the answer was plain. I finally discovered it; in verse 8 God tells Joshua, "This Book of the Law must not depart from your mouth. Meditate on it day and night so that you may act carefully according to all that is written in it. For then you will make your way successful, and you will be wise." Through in-depth meditation on God's promises, Joshua furthered his motivation by reinforcing the activity of his frontal lobes and his selective attention.

This same idea appears in Paul's epistle to the Romans, where the apostle declares that faith comes from what one "hears" from the Word of God. (See Romans 10:17.) In other words, what matters is giving sustained attention to what is heard—to examine it closely and understand it—than to simply listen to an announcement while a dozen other things float through your mind. Attentively listening, ruminating over a message, and sharpening it in your brain allows faith to blossom.

FIVE STEPS TO SUCCESSFUL MEDITATION

The studies carried out at the University of Philadelphia by Andrew Newberg and his team showed that spiritual experiences and the techniques used to achieve them involve a vast network of neural interconnections. Their research showed how these experiences are influenced by our thoughts, feelings, memories, genetic predisposition, life experiences, and physical condition. If we want to make the most of meditation and improve our brain function, we need to follow some steps to enhance daily practice:

- The first is a deep desire for change. What do we aspire to when we set aside time for meditation?

- Remain focused on the objective and avoid the habit of "intrusive thoughts." Namely, make an effort to prevent our minds from wandering and bringing us back to the previous day's trivialities or problems awaiting us.

- The more this activation is repeated over time, the stronger the cerebral connections grow.

- Voluntary regulation of breathing and deliberate relaxation of all muscle groups. This not only has a relaxing effect, it also reduces useless metabolic activities for the benefit of our hyperactive frontal lobes.

- The final step pertains to our faith or expectations. It is about our ability to believe that we are going to wait for the goals we have set and the inner conviction we will achieve them. In having this "confidence in what we hope for and assurance about what we do not see" (Heb. 11:1, NIV), we activate the motivation circuit and stimulate our immune system.[6]

Newberg emphasizes that faith is the best way to strengthen our brain, since it knows the assurance and belief that a happy future awaits God's children. Faith can be compared to optimism—a confidence that allows us to move forward despite life's uncertainties. In an article published in 2007 in the journal *Nature*, researchers from the National Institutes of Health demonstrated that—from a neurological point of view—a dose of optimism appears indispensable to maintaining motivation and mental health. They showed that the most optimistic persons have a particularly functional anterior cingulate gyrus.

Earlier I mentioned how this part of our brain is stimulated by meditative practices and plays an essential role in controlling negative emotions. Thus, meditation, through the anterior cingulate gyrus, increases our faith and strengthens positive emotions. A four-decade-long study at Duke University showed that optimistic individuals enjoyed greater longevity than pessimists. Others have demonstrated that optimism improves our ability to positively confront all kinds of diseases. Optimism appears so important from a medical and psychological point of view that the University of Pennsylvania created the Positive Psychology Center, exclusively dedicated to research in this field.

While essential to keeping the brain in a state of optimum shape, Newberg's research demonstrates how faith must be accompanied by spiritual exercises and a well-developed social life. In combining community activities, intellectual stimulation and faith, religious practice seems ideal to optimize cerebral functions.

Especially if we add the daily practice of meditation, just as the Bible—and now scientific research—encourages!

CREATING GOD?

Did God create the brain, or did our brain create God?

Neuroscience researcher Mario Beauregard posed that question in his 2007 book (coauthored with Denyse O'Leary), *The Spiritual Brain*. Beauregard, who holds a doctorate in neurobiology from the University of Texas, attracted international media coverage in 2008 for his claim that it is not the brain that creates the mind, but the mind that influences the brain. "Here is a key problem that must be addressed," the authors say. "Most of us, asked to give an account of ourselves, think that we have 'minds,' which we distinguish from our 'brains.' We consider that our minds generate the fundamental choice of action that the circuitry of our brains carries out. For example, a driver faced with an unexpected traffic jam may decide not to curse and hammer the horn, but simply to shrug and turn down a side street. We might describe the driver's thought process by saying, 'Harry made up his mind not to get upset, but not just go home another way.' We do not say, 'Harry's brain circuitry caused him to take his hand off the horn and instead steer the car to the right, down a side street.' We assume that Harry has free will, that he—or something in him—can really decide how we will act.... A materialist neuroscience cannot account for a mind or free will in this way. It assumes that Harry and any observers are the victims of an illusion of free will, because materialism has no model for how free will might actually work."[7]

Materialist neuroscientists think that what one calls the mind (self-awareness) is only the consequence of the electrical and chemical processes unfolding in our brain. Even more so, they believe mystical experiences may only be illusions fabricated by the activity of our neurons. Thus, it would simply be the human brain that could create these experiences and, finally, God. For these materialists, there thus exists no real spiritual source in mystical experiences.

Of course Beauregard doesn't support such a thesis: "Materialism is wrong in its assessment of human nature because it is not in accord with the evidence.... An open-minded neuroscience can significantly contribute to a model of mind (that is not a delusion) and tell us some important facts about spiritual/mystical experiences.... We now turn to our key question: What evidence from neuroscience casts doubt on a materialist interpretation of the human mind and spirituality?"[8]

Beauregard notably draws his conclusions from his research with Carmelite nuns from Montreal. The Carmelites—the most famous was Mother Teresa—devote much of their lives to meditation and prayer. Because of this, many undergo extraordinary mystical and spiritual experiences. Though they have varied ecstatic states, these experiences contain common characteristics. The subject most often declares his or her experience defies description, includes a state of "understanding," and is a process involving the whole self. It is not the kind of thing on which the intellect can form an opinion.

The goals of mystical experiences are transcendental and spiritual and never seem to explore or rearrange anything in the known universe. The subject expresses a living state of union with an entity lying beyond traditional consciousness—a being who is not only the reality of all that is, but is also an object of living and personal love, never an object of exploration. Obviously different authors have attempted to transform the ineffable into words, but they can offer only a glimpse of such experiences. Both rare and transitory, once they are gone, they can only be partially reproduced by memory.

Just like his colleague Newberg, Beauregard wanted to know what happened in the brain of these Carmelite sisters when they recalled a mystical experience, and what took place when they experienced one in real time. To accomplish this, he used functional magnetic resonance imaging and quantitative electroencephalography. Fifteen Carmelites, ranging in age from twenty-three to sixty-four, agreed to participate. All claimed to have at least one profound mystical experience. The goal of the study was to verify where the brain activity was located over the course of the mystical experience, and if it produced cerebral states not associated with ordinary consciousness.

In concrete terms two important things emerged from the trials. The first is that one can exclude the idea that a specific zone of the brain's temporal lobes exists—a sort of "God center." Previous theories endorsed the idea of a zone that allowed for explanation of spiritual experiences, even to produce and stimulate them. To the contrary, these studies showed that spiritual experiences correlate with the activation of different regions of the brain. These are usually involved in diverse functions, such as self-consciousness, emotions, and visual and motor imagery. The results revealed differences in the subjects' experiences as complex, multidimensional phenomena.

"The external reality of God cannot be directly proven or disproven by studying what happens to people's brains when they have mystical experiences," Beauregard wrote. "Demonstrating that specific brain states are associated with spiritual/mystical experiences neither shows that such experiences are 'nothing but' brain states nor proves that God exists. It shows only that it is reasonable to believe that mystics do contact a power outside themselves.... The fact that the human brain has a neurological substrate that enables it to experience a spiritual state can be construed as the gift of a divine creator or, if you prefer, as contact with the underlying nature or purpose of the universe. Materialist philosophers insist that such a substrate is meaningless and got there purely by chance. Nothing in the available scientific evidence requires that interpretation."[9]

THE MYSTICAL EXPERIENCE

When the nuns limited themselves to the memory of past experiences, their recorded brain activity differed from a mystical experience observed in real time. For Beauregard, there was no doubt that a mystical state is different from an ordinary emotional state. The recordings showed the nuns had a marked alteration of consciousness during their experiences. Moreover, thanks to the questionnaires and follow-up interviews, the nuns could distinguish between mystical experiences and simple recalling them. Certainly it remains impossible to prove through these experiences that mystical experiences are linked to "contact" with an outside force. Still, they allow for observation of a certain coherency between the recordings and the impact reported by those who had these experiences.

Furthermore, these observations showed that mystical experiences are not the result of particular genes or neurological disorders. To the contrary, those who experienced these encounters were typically healthy in body and mind. In addition, they cannot possibly be created or reproduced by just any technique. For Beauregard they are normal and correlate to physical and mental health because they express a natural, spiritual function. He also said that the difficult problem of consciousness is impossible to resolve within a purely materialistic framework: "Although one cannot demonstrate it, the data is consistent with an experience in which the subjects contact a spiritual reality independent of their own mind."[10]

This begs the question of whether these mystical experiences change just the lives of those who experience them, or the researchers as well. Some neuroscience researchers likely believe that man's brain is incapable of creating God. Others see it differently, such as Sir Alister Hardy (1896–1985). Oxford biologist and zoologist Hardy didn't just study biological systems. He wanted to learn more about these tough-to-explain spiritual experiences, albeit from a strictly Cartesian point of view. Hardy gathered and studied the accounts of mystics over a fifty-year period and opened a previously unexplored field of investigation. His work went against the grain of the reductionist, materialistic tendencies that prevailed in biology. Such views aimed to reduce mystical experiences to a dysfunction of the genes or neuron circuits.

But Hardy persisted, asking such questions as: Who goes through these experiences? Are they the same, according to cultures? What are they triggered by? What are their repercussions? He believed that if these experiences brought about something of the universe's true nature—and were inhabited by sense and purpose—they should make us feel like something more than evolved animals. To the contrary, he said they should make us feel that we are spiritual beings, bound to the source of our true nature. They should thus bring those who experience them empathy, the ability to feel united and in solidarity with others, and that they too are spiritual and sensitive beings in this dimension.

The work of Hardy and numerous other sources show how the major consequences of mystical experiences were bringing people a sense of purpose and meaning. Those who experienced them develop a more personally meaningful life and displayed a more compassionate attitude toward others. While Hardy did not look to demonstrate the truth of any religious doctrine, fifty years of studies and research brought him to the realization that humans are religious by nature. His irresistible and cross-cultural attraction to spirituality found its origins in this profound nature. Yet this truth was suffocated by the rhetoric and teachings of modern thinkers. How tragic.

Chapter 8

NOT ANY FAITH WILL DO

As he went he drew near Damascus, and suddenly a light from heaven shone around him. He fell to the ground and heard a voice saying to him, "Saul, Saul, why do you persecute Me?" He said, "Who are You, Lord?" The Lord said, "I am Jesus, whom you are persecuting. It is hard for you to kick against the goads." Trembling and astonished, he said, "Lord, what will You have me do?" The Lord said to him, "Rise up and go into the city, and you will be told what you must do."

—Acts 9:3–6

ALTHOUGH PRAYER AND faith can play a beneficial role in the individual's state of health, it would be an illusion to believe that all forms of spirituality are on equal footing. Certain religious practices can even be harmful. So in any discussion of religion or spirituality, someone is bound to ask: "What are we talking about?"

Beyond simple belief and membership in a domina-
tion or religious group—whether participating in public
religious activities or leaning toward a more personal
form of spirituality—motivation is a key ingredient of
such engagement. Defining spirituality's influence in a
person's life helps gauge what kind of difference this
makes in a person's life.

The psychologist Gordon Allport (1897–1967) did
extensive studies and writing about personality problems, particularly as they relate to religion. A Harvard
University professor, Allport was especially interested
in the concept of attitude. He examined this issue
from a more psychological and behavioral view, which
distanced him from the popular psychoanalytical
approach. Allport's 1950 book, *The Individual and His
Religion*, discussed various ways in which individuals
approach matters of faith.

Allport established a key distinction between *intrinsic*
and *extrinsic* spirituality. In his view persons with an
intrinsic spirituality are the most authentic. Their pursuit of spirituality comes from the inside. Motivated by
the heart, spirituality takes a central place in their life.
One could say that persons who embrace this form of
religion renounce themselves and turn to God. On the
other end of the scale are people with extrinsic motivation who use religion for the benefits they can derive
from it. Thus, religion occupies one place in their life
among many. They find religion "useful" because of the
sense of security it provides or the social relationships
it provides. Subjects with an extrinsic motivation supposedly turn to God, yet they never look away from self.

The distinction Allport proposed is reminiscent of the words of Jesus, when He warned His disciples "for whosoever shall desire to save his life shall lose it; and whosoever shall lose his life for my sake, he shall save it" (Luke 9:24, DARBY). When it comes to health, many scientific studies validate that those with an intrinsic faith reap the greatest benefits from spirituality. In his subsequent work, *The Nature of Prejudice* (1954), Allport reviewed how subjects with an intrinsic motivation are the most tolerant and least inclined toward interpersonal conflicts, a finding later confirmed by a series of studies in 2000–2002.[1]

This caring attitude toward others also brings health benefits. The words of the Apostle Paul, "Let all bitterness, wrath, anger, outbursts, and blasphemies, with all malice, be taken away from you. And be kind one to another, tenderhearted, forgiving one another, just as God in Christ also forgave you" (Eph. 4:31–32), are more than a Christian message of morality. They represent good health advice!

SPIRITUAL QUEST

The spiritual quest is another concept of religious pursuits. This term originated in the 1990s with Daniel Batson, a social psychologist of the University of Kansas. It concerned the personal aspects of research and the spiritual progression of an individual who informally possessed intrinsic religiosity. In addition to intrinsic and extrinsic motivation, Batson proposed a "third way." He defined this quest as a form of spirituality in which the questions are as important as the answers. The author wrote that these persons consider religion as an unlimited process of questionings and evaluations, generated by the tensions, contradictions and tragedies of their own lives, and of the society in which they evolve.[2]

Batson is among the many psychologists who have studied the phenomenon of empathy. He noted that people on a spiritual quest are inclined—more so than those of intrinsic orientation—to listen to the concerns of people needing help. Batson also showed how the act of "imagining oneself" in the place of a sufferer produces distress, while "imagining the other" in his needs cultivates a greater empathetic reaction and diminishes distress and discomfort.[3]

However, the most widespread religious experience, and that which moves across denominational divides, is that of conversion—often called the "new birth." (This term originates from the conversation between Jesus and Nicodemus, related in the third chapter of John.) This born-again conversion often leads to a change in aspirations, lifestyle, or personality. The most vivid example in biblical history is Saul, a noted persecutor of Christians. After being struck blind on the road to Damascus (in pursuit of Christians), Saul became the Apostle Paul and the most prolific author of the New Testament.

He wrote of his transformation:

> For you have heard of my former life in Judaism,
> how I persecuted the church of God beyond

measure and tried to destroy it, and progressed
in Judaism above many of my equals in my own
heritage, being more exceedingly zealous for the
traditions of my fathers. But when it pleased
God, who set me apart since I was in my mother's womb and called me by His grace, to reveal
His Son in me, that I might preach Him among
the nations, I did not immediately confer with
flesh and blood, nor did I go up to Jerusalem to
those who were apostles before me. But I went
into Arabia, and returned again to Damascus.

—GALATIANS 1:13–17

In another of his letters Paul wrote, "Therefore, if any
man is in Christ, he is a new creature. Old things have
passed away. Look, all things have become new" (2 Cor.
5:17). Such writings show how a conversion experience
can lead to emotional or physical recovery, or by deliverance from tobacco, alcohol, or drug addictions.

Writings throughout the ages offer additional
evidence. In his 1902 book, *Varieties of Religious
Experiences*, psychologist William James reported how
individuals had surprising religious experiences, such as
dramatic conversions, physical and emotional healings,
feelings of closeness to God or of becoming one with
Him, or entering another dimension of reality through
dreams or visions. A long-standing Christian tradition
of these types of experiences exists, be it through the
mysticism of Catholic saints, or more recently through
the exercise of spiritual gifts in Charismatic circles.

RELIGIOUS COPING

Religious coping refers to adapting to stress or difficulties through one's spiritual resources. This may include prayer or fasting to change one's outlook about tough circumstances, or to provide necessary emotional or mental resources. It embraces an attitude of "surrender to God" by letting go of self-directed efforts and trusting in divine Providence. It may include a conversation with a clergyperson or meditating on inspired texts to find comfort or alleviate anxiety. Numerous studies report close ties between such adaptation and intrinsic spirituality. Evaluating this phenomenon through questionnaires allows for two approaches:

- Collaborative—the subject and God work in partnership and are aware of what both parties must do to resolve the problem.

- Passive—the subject abandons his or her fortunes to Providence.

Researcher Kenneth Pargament has contributed the most insights to the study of this phenomenon. His 1997 book, *The Psychology of Religion and Coping: Theory, Research, Practice*, reviewed its importance in managing stress and preventing anxious states and depressive episodes. He particularly observed this beneficial role among patients suffering from various drug addictions, whether that meant preventing more serious intoxication or shedding the addiction. Another study published in 2000 showed that patients who adapt are more optimistic, receptive to social support during treatment with a more elevated level of resilience, and possess a lower anxiety level than subjects who did not take themselves into account or don't have any religious leanings.[4]

For those with an intrinsic spirituality, knowledge of God and His Word is of vital importance. Anyone who has spent time studying the Bible knows how, in the Old Testament, God repeatedly mentions turning away from His people if they ignore His precepts. The prophet Hosea expressed this aptly when he wrote, "My people are destroyed for lack of knowledge. Because you have rejected knowledge, I will reject you from being My priest. And because you have forgotten the law of your God, I will also forget your children" (Hosea 4:6).

Such knowledge is precious when it comes to successfully facing adverse circumstances, such as serious illness, since a biblically literate person is likely to possess a stronger faith. Paul likens the believer to a fighter: "Therefore put on the full armor of God, so that when the day of evil comes, you *may be able to* stand *your ground*, and after you have done everything, *to stand*" (Eph. 6:13, NIV, emphasis added). To take up this "armor" implies not only knowing God's Word, but also how to implement it in daily life. In such circumstances knowledge is more than theoretical. It contains a spiritual dimension.

Jesus warned against a theoretical faith. In His parable of the two houses, the house that fell was built on of sand—representing a believer who hears the Word but never puts it into practice. (See Matthew 7:24–27.) The person who builds on the rock, Jesus, uses the Word in daily life. Accumulating "bookish" knowledge without concrete application is risky. While it may offer temporary intellectual satisfaction, it will be of no help in the face of difficulty. James provided a recipe for happiness when he wrote, "Be doers of the word and not hearers only, *deceiving yourselves....* Whoever looks into the perfect law of liberty, and continues in it, and is not a forgetful hearer but *a doer of the work,* this man will be blessed in his deeds" (James 1:22, 25, emphasis added).

IMPLICATIONS OF FAITH

What are the implications of faith in daily life? In his letter to the Galatians, Paul spelled out the fruit of the Spirit that believers will see manifested in reality: "But the fruit of the Spirit is love, joy, peace, forbearance, kindness, goodness, faithfulness, gentleness and self-control" (Gal. 5:22–23, NIV). That says it all in a few words.

Ironically in recent years a number of works devoted to personal development have relied on such 2,000-year-old precepts. In his 2007 book, *Thanks! How the New Science of Gratitude Can Make You Happier,* psychology professor Robert Emmons wrote of the "new science of gratitude." That same year psychotherapist

Pierro Ferruci wrote a book-length exposition about the power of kindness and the benefits of compassion. Allan Luks and Peggy Payne discussed the healing power of benevolence in their 2001 book, *The Healing Power of Doing Good*. Medical professor Stephen Post explained how to live a longer and happier life by giving to others in *Why Good Things Happen to Good People* (2007). In *The Power of Giving* (2009) inspirational speaker Azim Jamal and fund-raising consultant Harvey McKinnon discussed the possibilities of creating abundance by simply giving to others.

Some of these works emphasize the biochemical modifications that occur in the brain when people engage in altruistic activity, such as lowering stress hormone production and increasing the secretion of endorphins. Thus, humans appear to be physiologically designed to function best when they are doing good. While the Bible already said this, over the years too many have relegated its teachings to strict lessons in morality. Twenty-first-century researchers have rediscovered these truths from another angle. (As Solomon wrote in Ecclesiastes 1:9, "There is nothing new under the sun.")

The publication of these and many other works is no coincidence. Our "enlightened" world appears to have lost contact with the essential goodness and virtues offered through spirituality and religion. The idea that belief can bring healing starts with the Holy Scriptures. Numerous critics of classic spirituality, whose voices are quite loud, typically emphasize the alienating aspects of religious extremism. In their eyes believers are neurotics and the well-being they sense an illusion. In short—to paraphrase Karl Marx—religion is the opium of a people who can find nothing better to help them swallow the bitter reality of existence.

RELIGION'S CRITICS

One of religion's most ferocious critics was Sigmund Freud, the aforementioned father of psychoanalysis. The Austrian psychiatrist cast religion and spirituality as the equivalent of neuroses, with roots in the Oedipus complex. More than a century ago, in his 1907 article, "Compulsive Actions and Religious Exercises," Freud compared religious rites with obsessive neuroses, relying on repression to curb natural urges. He accused religion of implementing guilt and anguish over imagined divine punishment. In his eyes faith spared people from the need to deal with the real source of their anxiety.

"Religion circumscribes these measures of choice and adaptation by urging upon everyone alike its single way of achieving happiness and guarding against pain," Freud wrote in *Civilization and Its Discontents*. "Its method consists in decrying the value of life and promulgating a view of the real world that is distorted like a delusion, and both of these imply a preliminary intimidating influence upon intelligence. At such a cost—by the forcible imposition of mental infantilism and inducing a mass delusion—religion succeeds in saving many people from individual neuroses. But little more."[5]

Freud refuted the value of faith because of his dislike for those whose dogmatic approach to religion forbad anyone from expressing a scintilla of doubt. To Freud, this posed impediments to free thought and kept individuals locked in infantile illusions to satisfy their neurotic needs. Ironically, this transformed Freud into a dogmatist himself. Instead of taking a critical (meaning scholarly) look at religion, he devoted himself to its systematic demolition. Like the spiritual practitioners he criticized, Freud's beliefs had consequences.

Others followed, such as American psychologist and influential psychotherapist Albert Ellis. A pioneer in cognitive behavioral therapies, in 1980 he wrote *The Case Against Religion*, in which he declared, "It is my contention that both pietistic theists and secular religionists—like virtually all people imbued with intense religiosity and fanaticism—are emotionally disturbed: usually neurotic and sometimes psychotic. For they strongly and rigidly believe in the same kinds of profound irrationalities, absolutistic musts, and unconditional necessities in which seriously disturbed people powerfully believe."[6] Later in the magazine *Free Inquiry* Ellis wrote an article describing eleven pathological traits common to religious persons, such as difficulties with self-acceptance, fanatic behavior, and problems establishing healthy relationships.

Granted, some of these observations are relevant. While these critiques may disturb some church members, they contain claims that believers must admit have some truthfulness. Ellis denounces a rigid certainty to faith and spirituality; we cannot deny such an approach exists. Yet I feel compelled to point out that this attitude, common among many believers, is the very one Jesus denounced! The outrageous, intolerant Pharisees (who still exist) and their smug self-righteousness were far from the values Christ extolled. Such views parallel the attitudes of fundamentalist and extremist followers of many other religions. From a psychological perspective, such attitudes have a detrimental impact on psychological and physical health.

What Conception of God?

A study in 2009 by researchers at the Swiss University of Zurich and Ruhr University Bochum in Germany looked at the religious feeling of psychological well-being. It showed that religion is not always comforting; in some cases it can contribute to the aggravation of psychological disorders or depression. Bernd Kräemer, head physician at the Polyclinic University of Zurich, noted that his team had thought of establishing a link between religious fervor and the ability to overcome hardships, but they were surprised to observe this was not always the case.

Researchers questioned 328 practicing Christians in Switzerland. These believers came from Reformed, Catholic, and Evangelical backgrounds who had endured recent hardships, such as social conflict, serious illness, trauma, or bereavement. As the interviews progressed, a disturbing fact emerged—suffering souls don't necessarily find gentleness and consolation from their faith. The scientists observed an indisputable relationship between a negative image of God and signs of depression, pain, and lack of well-being. In such cases no positive effects of religion emerged.

"We even have clear indications that a negative representation of God can lead to psychological problems," their report said. "In fact, the study shows that the persons who have a representation of a vengeful God have a tendency to consider the illness or loss of someone close as the punishment of their sins. Or they lament their fate: 'Why does God treat me in this fashion—me, who always obeyed the Christian precepts?' Moreover, the believers who received a religious education riddled by guilt may consider the loss of someone close as the punishment of their sins."[7]

God, gracious master or moral monster? Paul Copan tried to answer that question in his 2011 book, *Is God a Moral Monster?* This work was a response to a string of popular books written by so-called New Atheists, who portray the God of the Old Testament as a bully, murderer, and cosmic child abuser. It is not uncommon to encounter people—even Christians—who believe the Bible is culturally regressive, outdated, and opposed to basic human rights. Copan's book seeks to rehabilitate the public's ability to appreciate these texts. As he explains: "As we look at many of these Mosaic laws, we must appreciate them in their historical context, as God's gracious, temporary provision."[8]

While they may leave many unanswered questions, the Swiss and German researchers concluded that pastors and other caregivers should be more attentive to the images and representations of God their followers create. Their work shows that it is the conceptions of God that are at stake in the positive and negative reactions people exhibit in the face of traumatic life events.

MAKING ONE SICK?

Some works claim the constraining influence of faith and the church is behind some psychic disorders. They use such terms as "poisoning by God," "religious neurosis," "toxic faith," and "traumatizing upbringing." Critics question whether faith is a key factor in mental instability. Samuel Pfeifer, a psychiatrist and head physician of the Sonnenhalde Clinic near Bâsel, Switzerland, attempted to answer this in a book: *La Foi est-elle un Facteur de Déséquilibre?* (Is faith a factor of imbalance?). He examined how faith or piety can be a source of internal conflict and suffering. Pfeifer also examined to what extent a sensitive, neurotic personality influences spiritual experience, and the influence of Christian faith on a sensitive individual. Pfeiffer explained how neurotic conflict can be engendered by a tension between reality and religion's idealized view of existence. Every individual, believer or not, must take two realities into account:

- On one hand, the external framework that understands the environment in which the individual lives and his or

her rules and limits, and the person's
situation, social fabric, and physical
constitution—that is reality.

- On the other hand, the internal experience formed by the subject's ideals
(including political, ecological, personal,
or religious), and of his needs, feelings, and fundamental instincts—that is
the ideal.[9]

Every individual must navigate the tensions between
their ideals and external reality, find compromises
between needs and limits, and seek a reason for their
existence. The neurotic person may be considered as
someone who struggles to sanely manage these con-
flicting forces. Problems can occur when, in the context
of human tensions, religious elements adversely affect
a hypersensitive personality. However, this person may
already be inclined to a neurosis or mental disorder.

It seems that the image of God that individuals craft
for themselves is often at the heart of neuroses. The
Bible offers a wide range of ways in which men and
women experience a relationship with God. Pfeifer
showed that a person's image of God is a very personal
experience that reflects what the individual has experienced, as well as his or her hopes and fears. The author
explored how painful experiences, such as the death of
a loved one, can provoke conflict between ideals and
reality and prompt the question, "How can a good God
allow such a thing to happen?"

The way in which a person manages such cognitive dissonances depends on his or her ability to resolve physical conflicts. The author explained how—in neurotic persons—the experience results in a deformed image of God. Memories of sad experiences with their parents, humiliating situations at school, or fears of abandonment often play a key role. Combined with immaturity and a fearful approach to life, such individuals have a tendency to project their tensions and wounds on to God. Their simplistic conclusion is: "Because all this happened to me, God is cruel." A spiritual therapist seeks to help neurotic people form a new understanding of God—based on the Bible—and show them how a time of crisis is often an opportunity for growth. It can provoke the collapse of firmly anchored, outdated clichés and open a path to a new kind of divine encounter.

HARMFUL EFFECTS

Other negative consequences of religion on health exist. They fall under an erroneous approach to spirituality and a distorted reading of Scripture. Medical negligence is one that can have the most harmful consequences. To be clear: faith and spirituality are not intended to replace medical care, as shown by the following anecdote:

In his youth an old friend (now deceased) attended a meeting in Great Britain run by Smith Wigglesworth, a pioneer of the Pentecostal movement and known for spectacular healings during his meetings—and through his prayers.

"What are you suffering from?" Wigglesworth asked once my friend reached the front of the long line.

He responded, "From headaches."

"Well go home and take an aspirin and do not make me waste my time!" the evangelist replied rather harshly.

This illustrates that to believe in divine healing does not exclude treating oneself appropriately with an available remedy. Remember that while Jesus lived on this earth, patients often faced dire conditions that, thanks to today's medical progress, can be quickly healed. The woman with the issue of blood, who had exhausted all the natural recourses available before Jesus healed her, would likely be fine after a few weeks of taking progestin. (See Matthew 9:20–22.) The fever that floored Peter's mother-in-law would yield in a few hours to paracetamol and an antibiotic! (See Matthew 8:14–15.)

As for the "lunatics" and other epileptics Jesus delivered, today they would lead a more normal existence, thanks to psychotropic medications. Indeed, it is appalling in modern day to still hear certain extremist preachers encourage listeners to cease all medical treatment from the instant they trust in God's healing. It is simply criminal to encourage diabetics to interrupt insulin treatments, or manic-depressives to cease taking lithium. Many conditions are potentially devastating, meaning effective treatments are a valid option. I once met a paralyzed man now confined to a wheelchair and totally dependent. Why? Because one day he stopped taking his antidepressive medication upon the advice of a "man of God" who had prayed for his healing. A few days later, struggling with a suicidal compulsion, he threw himself out of a second-story window!

Such events rightly cast scorn on the faith and healing ministry, and discredit believers as a whole. In addition let us not forget that a large percentage of "miracles" offered as proof by evangelical faith healers is never documented. For a healing to be labeled "miraculous," the least one can expect is medical evidence that verifies the patient's condition before and after the so-called healing. Usually these illnesses are not as reported, nor is the healing necessarily a miracle. Or, at the least, it is difficult to attribute it solely to sovereign intervention.

The thirst for the miraculous that prevails in certain Charismatic and Pentecostal circles was denounced by international evangelist J. Lee Grady in his work *The Holy Spirit Is Not for Sale.* A Charismatic church member, for years the author was the privileged observer of certain deviations through his past duties as editor of the Christian magazine *Charisma.* He wrote, "The charismatic movement lost much in terms of credibility during the past few decades because we allowed imposters and charlatans to thrive in our midst. Some of these people started out with good intentions; many of them surely were anointed by the Holy Spirit's power in the beginning. But somewhere along the way, like Esau, they traded their birthright for a meager bowl of stew. They became enamored by the publicity or their big offerings, and before long any divine anointing they once had faded into a dim aura of self-importance."[10]

Still, do not each of us bear a responsibility for this sad situation? Through our thirst for the supernatural and spectacular, along with our propensity to think of God as a distributor of miracles, we miss the crux of the matter that can bring us well-being and good health: the development of an intimate, peaceful, and confident relationship with Jesus, "the author and finisher of our faith" (Heb. 12:2).

IGNORING TREATMENT

There is another aspect of medical negligence that can put the life of a believer in danger—relying solely on prayer for healing. To those who follow such a course, using any form of therapeutic care appears to constitute a lack of faith. This attitude can lead to diagnostic and treatment delays for symptoms that need immediate, specialized care. This can result in a lost chance for the patient, and in the most severe cases can be fatal.

In 1988 the *Journal of the American Medical Association* (JAMA) detailed a study at Eastern Carolina University in Greenville, South Carolina. It sought to examine why breast cancer mortality in the US is much higher among black women than whites. The study revealed how a determining element was the stage of cancer at the beginning of care. The researchers were able to bring to light that cultural beliefs were a strong indicator of how advanced the cancer would be at diagnosis. Among them were such fundamentalist beliefs as: "It's Satan who causes cancer," or, "If someone prays, God will heal her of cancer without treatment." Researchers have identified the same harmful, "faith only" effects regarding the belated treatment of AIDS.

Such a fundamentalist approach to spirituality and health has a negative impact. It leads to neglecting other, more rational and effective approaches. Yet certain followers reject medical treatments that don't appear to be "spiritual," or that they think will reflect a lack of faith. Sometimes the fear originates with reprisals from friends or family members who reason that—with just enough faith—the patient can be healed.

Yet we see such behavior among various backgrounds. Examples include the refusal of blood transfusions (Jehovah's Witnesses), vaccinations (Amish), or medical assistance in childbirth and newborn care (emphasized by a fundamentalist church in Indiana that has since collapsed). There is a clear risk for those who follow the extreme philosophy of leaders such as the founder of one fundamentalist sect in the Midwest who declared that Satan controls our natural world. Whether visible and accessible to the senses, in his eyes (whether science or education in general) medicine represented an occult force through which the "prince of this world" acts. How sad.

Other religious groups encourage and justify poor treatment of their followers, especially children. In 1995 Bette Bottoms, a professor of psychology at the University of Chicago, and her associates published "In the Name of God: A Profile of Religion-Related Child

Abuse" in the *Journal of Social Issues*. In this study she described cases where children were deprived of all medical care for religious reasons, and abuses perpetrated by the clergy to exorcize their supposed demons. These abuses went as far as acts of ritual torture on minors whom spiritual leaders considered impure.[11]

When it comes to psychiatric treatments, there is particularly a widespread distrust in Christian circles. Often considered incompatible with faith, certain Christian authors suggest to avoid all forms of psychotherapy, even those using a Christian approach. One couple invented the term "psychoheresy" to refer to Christian therapists and all forms of spiritual counseling. As with other physical health issues, a rigid and dogmatic attitude can lead to diagnostic delays and the use of effective treatment for cases of such illnesses.

These studies about the relationship between health and spirituality show that it is not an issue of faith as much as what we believe, that makes the difference. The image that the individual has of God plays a crucial role here. Surveys show that those who view God as a distant, vengeful, and punishing being see few health benefits from their faith, compared to those who consider God as loving, inclusive, and merciful (the biblical view). Certain research also shows that attributing health problems to demonic powers is associated with poorer mental health.

Nevertheless, these works do not allow for knowing if it is beliefs that disrupt mental health, or psychological deterioration that leads to extreme beliefs. In addition, participating in "confining" or coercive forms of spirituality produces a negative impact, from both a physical and psychological point of view. Indeed, commitment to sectarian systems frequently results in a trend toward previously described medical negligence. In addition, it goes together with a wide range of psychological and social disturbances, such as retreating into one's self, personality disorders, or delusions of persecution. However, these observations do not allow one to distinguish if these types of subjects are attracted by the sectarian systems, or if it is the systems that produce the disorders. In any case be aware that rigid certainty about matters of faith can be a sign of weakness, not strength.

CHAPTER 9

THE VIRTUES OF
CHRISTIAN CHARACTER

One gives freely, yet grows all the richer; another
withholds what he should give, and only suffers
want. Whoever brings blessing will be enriched,
and one who waters will himself be watered.

—PROVERBS 11:24-25, ESV

S PEAKING STRICTLY FROM a psychological
point of view, Christian values of altruism,
generosity, forgiveness, and acceptance offer considerable benefits. So many that such ideals generated more
studies and publications than can be easily numbered.

As an example, American economist Arthur Brooks,
president of the American Enterprise Institute, is one
of numerous authors who have address the benefits
of philanthropy. In his 2008 book, *Gross National
Happiness*, Brooks analyzed happiness factors in the

United States. He didn't beat around the bush: for him, happiness is like anything else—it's bought. Beyond this provocative formula, Brooks explains how time, effort, and money invested in something produce happiness. In other words, give, and you shall receive! This affirms the "Mother Teresa Effect"—the idea that generous people are happier than the stingy, because generosity cultivates positive emotions. According to the author, those who give have (precisely) a 33 percent higher likelihood of being happy than those who do not![1]

It's Good to Be Good!

In their 1991 book, *The Healing Powers of Doing Good*, health expert Allan Luks and coauthor Peggy Payne recapped studies of more than three thousand volunteers. His surveys showed that people who help others receive "the giver's high." Its feelings of plenitude, well-being, energy, and euphoria linger, boosting long-term health. The euphoria sensed after engaging in acts of charity corresponds to the release of endorphins in the brain, followed by a long period of calm and well-being. When volunteers recalled charitable acts, it presented benefits several hours or even days later.

Luks said such generosity also exerts beneficial effects on health in significantly reducing anxiety and depressive disorders, creating stronger social ties, and reducing negative emotions such as feelings of isolation or hostility, which can release stress hormones and lead to psychological disorders. These diverse effects help strengthen the immune system and reduce susceptibility to diseases. For the author, to participate in acts of kindness would be the "happiness equivalent" of passing an exam or receiving a substantial increase in salary.

In *Why Good Things Happen to Good People* psychologist Stephen Post reviewed a more detailed examination of the changes our brain undergoes when we serve others. A professor of bioethics and family therapy at Cleveland's Case Western Reserve University, Post said the adoption of altruistic behaviors modifies our neuronal connections. His conclusions stem from a review of studies, including one involving a fifty-year-long follow-up period. It demonstrated that those who give of themselves during their high school years enjoy better physical and mental health throughout life. Another study Post reviewed came from Doug Oman at the University of California at Berkeley. Oman studied more than two thousand people over the age of fifty-five who were involved in humanitarian and voluntary service. He showed that they enjoyed a 44 percent reduction in mortality rates—in other words, just short of that of quitting smoking!

Moreover, according to Marc Musick of the University of Texas, subjects who take care of others live longer and better lives, regardless of the helper's age. Altruistic behaviors appear quite beneficial to young people, reducing their risks for depression and suicide. Generous adolescents are more optimistic, better socially integrated, happier, and more engaged than the average young person. Generosity also seems to be a good bulwark against stress and anxiety. Over a three-year period Neal Krause of the University of Michigan studied nearly one thousand religious individuals who were committed to their churches. Their engagement in social action with others helped those stuck in delicate economic situations to feel less anxious. Helping others is equally beneficial for those who suffer from chronic illnesses, such as multiple sclerosis, heart disorders, or HIV infection.

Finally these studies also showed that those who help their neighbor are happier. For example, to pray for others cushions the impact of health problems during one's senior years. A study of the National Institutes of Health showed that the simple act of thinking about making a charitable donation allows for the increase of dopamine, sometimes called the "hormone of happiness." What's more, a Harvard University study showed the simple act of watching a film that speaks of generosity and altruism strengthens the immune system.

GIVING HOPE

Jill Neimark, the journalist who coauthored *Why Good Things Happen to Good People,* related her own story in the book. Because of a tick bite, she suffered from Lyme disease, which caused her pain and chronic fatigue during the research and writing of the book.

"When I met Stephen in 2003, I was in the midst of my own singular hell," Neimark wrote. "Three years earlier I'd been bitten by a tick, and I've struggled mightily ever since with what is informally known as Lyme disease, an endless tedium marked by pain and exhaustion. Chronic illness shutters your world and whittles away at your whimsy, rapture, faith, and most of all, your own innate goodness. I needed to find a way back to myself. What I found stunning was that evolution had so clearly hardwired helpfulness into our genetic legacy. Young or old, sick or well, married or single, giving shines an amazingly beneficent, protective light on the giver. But science, no matter how impeccable, doesn't necessarily stir the heart. It was the real stories from real lives that breathed hope back into me."[2]

Reverend Otis Moss Jr., a disciple of Dr. Martin Luther King Jr., and author of the book's preface, concluded with this suggestion: "When you are in a desert, plant a rose. Plant a rose of liberation. Plant a rose of peace, a rose of reconciliation and a rose of faith, hope, and love. And the desert will blossom."[3] Such advice reflects the words of Jesus, who encouraged His disciples to be generous and magnanimous: "Be therefore merciful, even as your Father is merciful.... Give, and it will be given to you: Good measure, pressed down, shaken together, and running over will men give unto you. For with the measure you use, it will be measured unto you" (Luke 6:36–38).

Ignoring these truths results in an ever-increasing amount of negative headlines, which reminds us that withdrawing into self—whether because of fear of others or inordinate self-centeredness—comes at a high price. It particularly robs us of the chance to find lasting satisfaction in life. Granted there are still people driven by a sense of generosity and altruism, but in daily life the presence of self-interest has helped erode civility, good manners, and concern for others. Lest you think I exaggerate, the problem is so bad that in France, we see the need to celebrate "World Kindness Day" (May 10), "World Friendship Day" (October 25), and even "World Hug Day" (the first Saturday of July)! Among other national campaigns in recent times are the fight against loneliness (2011), the fight against violence toward women (2010), boosting organ donation (2009), and improving fraternity (2004). Then there is "free hug" trend, where individuals freely offer to take you in their arms.

Ice Age of the Heart?

All this goes to show that what came naturally not so long ago is now considered exceptional, to the point that we feel the need to create special events to remember acts of kindness. This evolution doesn't surprise students of the Bible. During His time on the earth Jesus warned: "Because of the increase of wickedness, the love of most will grow cold" (Matt. 24:12, NIV). In his first letter to his protégé, Timothy, Paul warned of the fading of love: "Know this: In the last days perilous times will come. Men will be lovers of themselves, lovers of money, boastful, proud, blasphemers, disobedient to parents, unthankful, unholy, without natural affection, trucebreakers, slanderers, unrestrained, fierce, despisers of those who are good, traitors, reckless, conceited, lovers of pleasures more than lovers of God, having a form of godliness, but denying its power" (2 Tim. 3:1–5).

If happiness and serenity depend on generosity and faith, it shouldn't surprise anyone that stress and anxiety have assumed epidemic-sized proportions in "advanced" societies. People in Western nations constantly consume antianxiety agents and antidepressants, often resorting to them at the slightest sign of difficulty. Certainly such medications offer a service to unhappy people, but let us not forget what makes up the essence of a healthy society: sharing, solidarity, friendship, and self-sacrifice. We need to rediscover and practice the kind of virtues that, ultimately, will benefit us!

In his 2007 book, *The Power of Kindness: The Unexpected Benefits of Leading a Compassionate Life*, Italian psychotherapist Piero Ferrucci chronicled how modern society is entering a sort of "ice age of the heart," seen through a growing indifference to one another. So gradual it has happened almost unnoticeably, one-on-one contact has been replaced by "virtual relationships" and social networks. While this may seem like no big deal, this kind of environment creates strained relationships in the workplace. Instead of collaborators, people turn into rivals, with solidarity giving way to the evolutionary ethic of "every man for himself." People strive against each other in hopes of gaining a promotion or just keeping their place, often to the detriment of another. The relentless pursuit of gain at all costs and rampant consumerism engulfs our existence. When coldheartedness reigns, it diminishes the values and common purpose that build society and provide people direction.

As a remedy for our discontent, Ferrucci proposed reinstating kindness as the priority in life. He argued that kindness can become a habit that not only does good to others, but also to those who practice it. This psychotherapist's work, which became a major reference point, generated acclaim after its publication. And yet, a few centuries earlier Paul had passed on these precepts to the disciples at Ephesus: "Let all bitterness, wrath, anger, outbursts, and blasphemies, with all malice, be taken away from you. And be kind one to another, tenderhearted, forgiving one another, just as God in Christ also forgave you" (Eph. 4:31–32).

Some want to interpret Paul's (and other biblical writers) recommendations as some kind of moralistic standard, one to which believers *must* conform to at the risk of incurring God's wrath. However, what if we see them as "recipes" for happiness prompted by the Holy Spirit? Professionals of the psyche need to get involved in spiritual discussions to ensure that millions can rediscover the value of biblical precepts. They are not so much moral rulers as life principles—guidelines that will bless our lives, individually and collectively.

Many theorize that we are happiest when we are the object of others' attention. In fact, the opposite is true. As Ferrucci wrote, "Giving kindness does us as much good as receiving it.... You can safely say—and scientific research confirms it—that kind people are healthier and live longer, are more popular and productive, have greater success in business, and are happier than others. In other words, they are destined to live a much more interesting and fulfilling life than those who lack this quality."[4]

Ferrucci makes the distinction between an authentic and interested attitude and the kind of calculated cunning that engages in service while secretly embracing ulterior motives. He added, "Suppose we are kind in order to feel better and live longer. Wouldn't be perverting the very nature of kindness? We would make it calculated and self-interested, and therefore it would no longer be kindness. How true! Kindness derives its purpose from itself, not from other motives. The true benefit of kindness is being kind. Perhaps more than any other factor, kindness gives meaning and value to our life, raises us above our troubles and our battles, and makes us feel good about ourselves."[5]

BE THANKFUL!

Although Paul exhorted Christ's followers long ago in Colossians 3:15 to be thankful, today science also encourages displays of gratitude. Robert Emmons, whom I mentioned in the last chapter, conducted the first broad-ranging scientific study of the impact of gratitude on health and quality of life. His aforementioned book, *Thanks!*, showed how thankful people derive benefits from increases in positive emotions such as joy, enthusiasm, love, and optimism. Applying

these virtues protects against such destructive tendencies as jealousy, covetousness, bitterness, and
resentment. A grateful person makes the best of life
and demonstrates resilience in spite of hard knocks.
Such people are liable to heal faster from disease,
enjoy a better level of health, and reap other benefits,
Emmons said. According to his research, gratitude
is essential to experiencing pleasure and recognizing
our dependency on others protects us against frustration engendered by our consumer-oriented society.

Emmons also showed how ingratitude can harm
psychological balance and damage our overall health.
The tendency to compare ourselves to others or cast
ourselves in a "victim" role promotes wallowing in self-
pity and emotional conflict. Emmons was particularly
affected by individuals who expressed gratitude for
little things, even when beset by great torments. They
transformed adversity into an opportunity to learn
about themselves and others. This reflects the advice of
the Apostle James: "My brothers, count it all joy when
you fall into diverse temptations, knowing that the
trying of your faith develops patience" (James 1:2–3).

Faith in a God who transcends our happenings and
yet continually watches over us helps us stand firm and
enables us to find glimmers of light amid life's darkness.
Like forgiveness, gratitude is a conscious choice rather
than a passive feeling. We can deliberately choose to
be thankful, even when emotions and feelings attempt
to do us harm. When we deliberately adopt a grateful
attitude despite adverse circumstances, it is surprising
how many opportunities present themselves to us to

express thankfulness instead of sinking into self-pity. For example, we can choose gratitude in the face of harsh criticism that otherwise can stir bitterness in our hearts, just as we can opt to forgive when our natural impulse is to seek revenge and reparations!

None of this is to pretend virtue comes easy. As Emmons acknowledged, this feeling is not inherently natural: "Gratitude can be a bitter pill to swallow, humbling us and demanding as it does that we confront our own sense of self-sufficiency.... Far from being a warm, fuzzy sentiment, gratitude is morally and intellectually demanding."[6] And as Emmons notes, gratitude has a difficult time in a culture that celebrates conspicuous consumption and ego. Gratitude is only one option among an array of responses: "What does it mean that gratitude is a choice? It means that we sharpen our ability to recognize and acknowledge the giftedness of life. It means that we make a conscious decision to see blessings instead of curses. It means that our internal reactions are not determined by external forces."[7]

Those who look to put their faith into practice will inevitably face the challenge of expressing gratitude when circumstances demand otherwise. Not only can we look to the Bible as our guide, Emmons' work also helps us recognize the benefits we will see when it comes to our health. So does that of other authors. In his famed 1980 book, *Power in Praise*, Merlin Carothers proposed adopting an attitude of praise and thankfulness to God, regardless of life's circumstances. While this may seem evident when all is well, it poses a much more difficult—even unnatural—obstacle when life hands us a bitter pill. Nevertheless that is what the Bible encourages:

> In everything give thanks, for this is the will of God in Christ Jesus concerning you.
> —1 THESSALONIANS 5:18

> Rejoice in the Lord always. Again I will say, rejoice!
> —PHILIPPIANS 4:4

> Give thanks always for all things to God the Father in the name of our Lord Jesus Christ.
> —EPHESIANS 5:20

AS WE FORGIVE

One day Peter, one of Jesus's first disciples, approached his Master to ask how many times he should pardon someone who offended him. Peter suggested the answer: seven times seemed sufficient to satisfy the requirements for good reciprocal relationships. But Jesus replied, "I do not say to you up to seven times, but up to seventy times seven" (Matt. 18:22). Imagine that. Have you ever been asked to forgive someone who has harmed you 490 times? By suggesting such a far-ranging response (which most consider excessive), Jesus indicated the extent of His forgiveness. It was only one of the Lord's numerous exhortations about forgiveness. He taught in the Lord's Prayer that we should ask the Father to "forgive us our debts, as we forgive our debtors" (Matt. 6:12). Likewise, Paul wrote to the church at Colosse: "Bear with one another and forgive one another. If anyone has a quarrel against anyone, even as Christ forgave you, so you must do" (Col. 3:13).

The issue of forgiveness is central to numerous religions, Christianity in particular. It is also one of the most studied aspects in modern psychology after being practically ignored by researchers in the 1980s. These numerous studies show that forgiveness is essential for health, be it spiritual, psychological, or even physical. (I will not restate here the significant spiritual benefits of forgiveness; for a closer examination see *Total Forgiveness* by R. T. Kendall, one of the best on the subject.)

Forgiveness has merited so much literature that I can only recap a few of the books and studies. In the *Handbook of the Psychology of Religion and Spirituality* editors Raymond Paloutzian and Crystal Park include an entire chapter—written by Michael McCullough, Giacomo Bono, and Lindsey Root—on forgiveness and its relationships with psychological and physical health. The authors first attempted to answer the question: "What is forgiveness?" While their exploration consists of examining attitudes using psychological definitions, they nevertheless shed light upon the profound nature of this internal disposition.

Forgiveness is of such interest that Robert Enright, a professor of psychology at the University of Wisconsin, founded the International Forgiveness Institute. For this specialist forgiveness is far-reaching and differentiates itself from simple reconciliation;

the latter defines itself as restoring confidence and mutual relationships. Yet it is possible to forgive persons with whom all restoration of a relationship has become impossible (such as a deceased person), or where a personal confrontation may be undesirable.[8] Specialists generally agree with this approach.

On the other hand, the opinions on the psychological nature of forgiveness vary. Enright would say, "Forgiveness is a choice," the title of his 2001 book published by the American Psychology Association. In his eyes it occurs when victims of a transgression are able to treat the aggressor with compassion, leniency, and affection while abandoning their rights to harbor negative feelings against that individual. Professor Everett Worthington, author of *Five Steps to Forgiveness*, wrote that when an individual is in a dynamic of forgiveness, positive emotions (i.e., empathy, compassion, sympathy) replace the initial, negative impulses toward the transgressor. University of Miami psychology professor Michael McCullough, the author of numerous works and articles on forgiveness and gratitude, sees forgiveness as a process. He says it starts when the desire to avoid the person who harmed you, or to avenge yourself, gives way to more lenient feelings.

IMPROVED HEALTH

Whatever the nuances identified by researchers, the body of their work indicates that forgiveness is associated with improved physical and psychological health.

For some the propensity to forgive—more frequent in those who possess an intrinsic spirituality—is a principal benefit. Conversely researchers point out that an inflexible, vindictive temperament increases the risk of a heart attack and increased cortisol secretion. Known as the "stress hormone," higher levels of cortisol can contribute to such conditions as blood sugar imbalances and diabetes, obesity, inflammation, gastrointestinal problems, and a weakened immune system.

To better gauge the impact of forgiveness, a team led by psychology professor Charlotte Witvliet studied volunteers who were asked to look back on an insult and consider four kinds of thought about the offender:

- Rancor
- A desire for revenge
- Empathy toward the person behind the insult
- Thoughts of forgiveness

The researchers discovered that when they fed participants thoughts of rancor or revenge, the subjects displayed increased facial muscle tension, and experienced elevated blood pressure and heart rate. These physiological modifications paralleled negative emotions felt by other participants of the study who were sad, angry, or sensed a loss of control. In addition, these negative feelings persisted after researchers told the volunteers to cease thinking about rancor or revenge. The researchers concluded that maintaining a persistent attitude of unforgiveness can adversely affect the person's health, most notably the cardiovascular system.

Other researchers highlighted how forgiving others can have positive effects on psychological well-being. All of the studies examining forgiveness showed how those who readily forgive experience reduced anxiety and depressive disorders, and improved levels of self-confidence and hope. Several studies proved that a correlation existed between the ease of forgiving an individual and spiritual well-being.[9]

Such studies show clear links between spirituality and attitudes of forgiveness, generosity, thankfulness, and empathy. The association between these positive feelings and markers of health and psychological well-being indicate that the beneficial influence of religion on health depends largely on "Christian character." If we are honest and forthright about the topic of human nature, we will admit that—without a counterbalancing influence—people are inclined toward self-centeredness, wickedness, and revenge. What's more, we are more apt to spontaneously feed these negative feelings. This is why the Bible tells us to allow God's Word to transform and change our thinking and natural human inclinations. We can see this advice in such passages as:

> But you did not learn about Christ in this manner,
> if indeed you have heard Him and have been
> taught by Him, as the truth is in Jesus: that you
> put off the former way of life in the old nature,

which is corrupt according to the deceitful lusts, and be renewed in the spirit of your mind; and that you put on the new nature, which was created according to God in righteousness and true holiness.

—EPHESIANS 4:20–24

So embrace, as the elect of God, holy and beloved, a spirit of mercy, kindness, humbleness of mind, meekness, and longsuffering. Bear with one another and forgive one another. If anyone has a quarrel against anyone, even as Christ forgave you, so you must do.

—COLOSSIANS 3:12–13

And when you stand praying, forgive if you have anything against anyone, so that your Father who is in heaven may also forgive you your sins.

—MARK 11:25

Christ's followers believe that the Spirit of God is able to accomplish what otherwise would be impossible. Namely, to change our old, self-directed, destructive nature with all its cravings and bad desires, and transform it into one of compassion, humility, patience, and gentleness, reborn in the image of the master, Jesus. This not only creates better individuals, it also is a blessing to society.

CHAPTER 10

AN INTIMATE GOD

O LORD, you have searched me and known me!
You know when I sit down and when I rise up; you
discern my thoughts from afar. You search out
my path and my lying down and are acquainted
with all my ways. Even before a word is on my
tongue, behold, O LORD, you know it altogether.

—PSALM 139:1–4, ESV

WITH THIS CHAPTER we come to the last and most practical section of this book. In previous chapters I observed how the image—for better or worse—we develop of God is vital to good health. Thus, in order to draw the greatest benefit from one's faith in terms of health, it is essential to possess knowledge of God as revealed in the Bible. It is also the responsibility of pastors and those who teach the Bible to communicate the love and forgiveness of God to all who wish to draw near to Him. This chapter is intended to remind readers what the Bible says about God and encourage believers to develop an intrinsic spirituality. That is to say, to develop the kind of personal intimate relationship with Him that helps you to trust in Him and expect the fulfillment of His promises. I hope you will also tell others, as Christ did in His prayer in the Garden of Gethsemane: "This is eternal life: that they may know You, the only true God, and Jesus Christ, whom You have sent" (John 17:3).

As mentioned previously, when it comes to health, intrinsic spirituality is the most beneficial. When our primary motivation originates with faith, it will bring other aspects of life into harmony with this foundation. We will go through life asking God what we can give to others and do for them, instead of constantly seeking to get something from them. We will have the kind of intrinsic outlook Gordon Allport (whom I mentioned in chapter 8) defined. We won't seek to put on a religious show, but embrace an authentic faith. We won't worry about how others see us, but what God thinks. We will seek to carry out His plans, not our agendas.

SHUT THE DOOR AND PRAY

Religious displays that only last until the spotlight is off are dangerous. The Gospel of Matthew describes how Jesus cautioned His disciples against seeking intimacy with God through public demonstrations instead of private, one-on-one prayer: "When you pray, you shall not be like the hypocrites. For they love to pray standing in the synagogues and on the street corners that they may be seen by men. Truly I say to you, they have their reward. But you, when you pray, enter your closet, and when you have shut your door, pray to your Father who is in secret. And your Father who sees in secret will reward you openly" (Matt. 6:5–6).

Note that Jesus said to "pray to your Father," not "pray to God" or "pray to the eternal Lord;" the latter two would have conformed to that era's religious traditions. This phrase showed the degree of intimacy with God Jesus invited His disciples to enjoy—a departure from religious norms. Praying in the privacy of one's room is quite different from praying in the sight of others. This call to intimacy tells us how important it is to know the One we are addressing. He alone is the One who sees us and hears our petitions.

Paul reflected this call to intimate prayer in his letter to the Ephesians: "Therefore I also, after hearing of your faith in the Lord Jesus and your love toward all the saints, do not cease giving thanks for you, mentioning you in my prayers, so that the God of our Lord Jesus Christ, the Father of glory, may give you the Spirit of wisdom and revelation in the knowledge of Him, that the eyes of your understanding may be enlightened, that you may know what is the hope of His calling and what are the riches of the glory of His inheritance among the saints, and what is the surpassing greatness of His power toward us who believe" (Eph. 1:15–19).

The apostle prayed that, through His Spirit, God would communicate wisdom and revelation to the Ephesians so they would know Him on a deep level and all the blessings that come with this kind of intimacy. This passage shows the explicit importance the apostle assigned to his relationship with God. Paul wanted the church at Ephesus (and, by extension, all Christians who would follow) to know God as He is and not as we would like to imagine Him.

CREATED IN MANKIND'S IMAGE

Throughout history humans have displayed the tendency to fashion their own ideas of God. Most of the time they arise from personal aspirations, suit mankind's ideas of how God should act, or conform to a human reference system. Many people reason: "God should be like this or like that. He should follow our desires or our needs, according to what we can accept or understand." This habit appeared in the episode of the golden calf built by the children of Israel in the wilderness, after they escaped from Egypt. When Moses left the Israelites to meet with God on the mountain, the people grew impatient and demanded of Aaron, "Come, make us gods which will go before us. As for this Moses, the man who brought us up out of the land of Egypt, we do not know what has become of him" (Exod. 32:1).

Cowed by the crowd before him, Aaron obeyed, collected gold earrings, and fashioned them into a golden statue vaguely resembling Apis, the Egyptian god of fertility and fecundity. The people responded: "This is your god, O Israel, who brought you up from the land of Egypt" (Exod. 32:4). (Then, to compound his mistake of bowing to the people's demands, Aaron followed up by building an altar to it and declaring the next day a feast day).

However, the God of the Bible does not come in small, prefabricated packages. The concepts people invent rarely correspond to the God who reveals Himself in the Scriptures. This raises the question: Is it possible to attain an objective and personal understanding of God and of the Bible? For J. I. Packer, who wrote the international best seller *Knowing God*, it is necessary to begin with the study of God. However, Packer says that accurate theology mustn't be an overarching goal. He says we must embrace a theoretical and scientific knowledge of God if we hope to possess a practical, intimate knowledge of Him. For this Packer says we must meditate on each biblical truth as we seek God and learn the power of prayer and praise.

Taste and See

A comprehensive knowledge of your spouse's family tree, background, and accomplishments won't guarantee marital bliss. Finding happiness requires the experience of a shared life. Only constant conversation, exchanges of views, and personal interaction help to build a solid, long-lasting, and satisfying marital relationship. The same applies to our personal relationship with God. As David wrote in the Psalms, "Oh, taste and see that the Lord is good; blessed is the man who takes refuge in Him" (Ps. 34:8). In less than twenty words David delivers the essence of a good spiritual life.

Our destination should be entering into God's presence and remaining there. Within Him we can find happiness, fulfillment, and security, which is the central point of Christianity. This is what Jesus and other biblical authors invited people to seek. Earlier in Psalm 34 David personalized the blessings he experienced in relating to God's presence: "I sought the LORD, and He answered me, and delivered me from all my fears. They looked to Him and became radiant, and their faces are not ashamed. This poor man cried, and the LORD heard, and saved him out of all his troubles" (Ps. 34:4–6). David's words offer a beautiful example of intrinsic spirituality's blessings. There is no doubt that those who liberate their fears and radiate with joy are in much better shape than persons consumed with worry and doubts about the future. Only those who experience a personal and meaningful relationship with God can appreciate the extent of God's availability to those who seek Him.

We can see a striking biblical example of this in Genesis, when Adam and Eve disobeyed God and ate of the tree of the knowledge of good and evil. Afraid of what might happen, they hid in the Garden of Eden. Yet God came looking for them: "The LORD God called to the man and said to him, 'Where are you?' He [Adam] said, "I heard Your voice in the garden and was afraid because I was naked, *so I hid myself*" (Gen. 3:9–10, emphasis added).

God searching for Adam and Eve after they disobeyed Him reveals how God has never hidden Himself from mankind. God never caused the break that occurred because of the first humans' disobedience. We are only separated from God when we refuse His counsel and harbor attitudes of selfishness and rebellion. God desires to reveal Himself, but in hiding we embrace pretexts stemming from the fruit of human-centered intelligence. In consuming the fruit of the tree of the knowledge of good and evil—knowledge that was not part of God's plan—mankind consumed faulty reasoning about our relationship with God.

However, although Adam and Eve's original sin changed mankind's heart, it did not change God's. Ever since the day of separation in the Garden of Eden, God has been at work to reveal the desires of His heart and love for His crowning creation. When the Apostle Paul addressed those who do not know God, he warned that Christ's followers should "walk not as other Gentiles walk, in the vanity of their minds, having their understanding darkened, excluded from the life of God through the ignorance that is within them, due to the hardness of their hearts" (Eph. 4:17–18). It is because of ignorance and distorted intelligence that so many people have become incapable of understanding God's intentions, character, and everlasting goodness.

Despite this sad state God seeks to reveal Himself and enter into close communion with mankind. After Adam and Eve's fall, He began by forging an alliance with godly individuals, and then with the nation of Israel. He based His first covenant on a complex set of laws that ordinary mortals proved incapable of following. However, this law accomplished its purpose— to reveal the insurmountable gap separating God from human beings. Yet God didn't leave it at that. Through the prophet Jeremiah, He spoke of a new alliance destined to replace the old: "But this shall be the covenant that I will make with the house of Israel after those days, says the LORD: I will put My law within them and write it in their hearts; and I will be their God, and they shall be My people" (Jer. 31:33).

Those days of which the prophet spoke (which eventually gave way to a new covenant) consisted of a formal relationship, one based on a rigid, restrictive set of commandments. Yet God's heartfelt cry is obvious: "I will be their God, and they will be my people." Prior to the separation between God and mankind, the Scripture suggests that the Spirit of God was in man; as Genesis says, "Then the LORD said, 'My Spirit shall not abide in man forever, for he is flesh: his days shall be 120 years'" (Gen. 6:3, ESV). God's desire was the restoration of everything that existed prior to the separation with man.

This desire came to fruition on the day of Pentecost, during the outpouring of the Holy Spirit on the first church. On this day the words of the Old Testament prophet Joel came to pass. They are aptly described by Luke, the author of Acts: "But Peter, standing up with the eleven, lifted up his voice and said to them, 'Men of Judea and all you who dwell in Jerusalem, let this be known to you, and listen to my words. For these are not drunk, as you suppose, since it is the third hour of the day. But this is what was spoken by the prophet Joel: "In the last days it shall be," says God, "that I will pour out My Spirit on all flesh; your sons and your daughters shall prophesy, your young men shall see visions, and your old men shall dream dreams. Even on My menservants and maidservants I will pour out My Spirit in those days; and they shall prophesy"'" (Acts 2:14–18).

Set Apart

The Bible often compares the Holy Spirit to water that brings freshness and vitality in the midst of barrenness. But it also compares the Spirit to the anointing oil used to set apart the priests and kings in the Old Testament. Thus the Spirit is literally the Spirit of Sanctity, which makes people holy and sets them apart. We are not set "apart" for God's use in following the Law, but by receiving the Holy Spirit (God's primary objective). The primary function of the Spirit is to bestow on us the sanctity God requires. Without this sanctity, we cannot draw close to God. The Hebrew people did not succeed in attaining this sanctification through Moses's law. The only one able to accomplish this, thanks to His dual nature (fully human and fully divine) is Jesus. He is the only way to receive this sanctification, which we receive through the Holy Spirit.

Before He departed, Jesus told His disciples at the Last Supper this Spirit would reveal all we needed to know: "The Counselor, the Holy Spirit, whom the Father will send in My name, will teach you everything and remind you of all that I told you" (John 14:26). This is indeed a matter of the Law of God written in our hearts, on the tablets of human flesh, which is God's second objective. Later that evening, Jesus said, "All that the Father has is Mine. Therefore I said that He will take what is Mine and will declare it to you" (John 16:15).

So to know God, we need a revelation. The complete manifestation resides in the person of Jesus Christ. In *Knowing God* Packer wrote that we know someone to the degree they open up to us. And it is the person of Jesus that God opened up the most comprehensively to humanity. As John wrote, "No one has seen God at any time. The only Son, who is at the Father's side, has made Him known" (John 1:18).

GOD INCARNATE

John 14:5–10 contains this interesting dialogue between Jesus and His disciples, as Christ prepares them for His departure:

> Jesus: You know where I am going, and you know the way.
>
> Thomas: Lord, we do not know where You are going. How can we know the way?
>
> Jesus: I am the way, the truth, and the life. No one comes to the Father except through Me. If you had known Me, you would have known My Father also. From now on you do know Him and have seen Him.
>
> Philip: Lord, show us the Father, and that is sufficient for us.

Jesus: Have I been with you such a long time, and yet you have not known Me, Philip? He who has seen Me has seen the Father. So how can you say, "Show us the Father"? Do you not believe that I am in the Father and the Father is in Me? The words that I say to you I do not speak on My own authority. But the Father who lives in Me does the works.

God's choice—that we truly understand who He is—was to incarnate Himself in the form of the God-man Jesus, and to meet us on our level. He came that we might no longer be unable to approach a distant, remote, and impenetrable God. Paul wrote of this in his letters to the Colossians: "He is the image of the invisible God and the firstborn of every creature" (Col. 1:15), and to the Philippians: "He emptied Himself, taking upon Himself the form of a servant, and was made in the likeness of men. And being found in the form of a man, He humbled Himself and became obedient to death, even death on a cross" (Phil. 2:7–8). The writer of Hebrews further expounds on Christ's amazing mission: "God, who at various times and in diverse ways spoke long ago to the fathers through the prophets, has in these last days spoken to us by His Son, whom He has appointed heir of all things, and through whom He made the world. He is the brightness of His glory, the express image of Himself, and upholds all things by the word of His power" (Heb. 1:1–3).

This mystery of incarnation—God taking on the form of mankind—is explained by God's intention to reveal His person and intentions toward us. In other words, His love, goodness, and salvation. The key to lasting happiness is to know Him and walk alongside of Him. This is, David discovered, in spite of his serious flaws and murderous actions, and what he expressed so poetically in the Psalms.

This incarnation centers on the three persons who collaborate in the Trinity:

- The Father, who expresses His intentions of salvation for humanity

- The Son, who embodies those intentions here, in our earthly reality

- The Holy Spirit, who is constantly at work to carry out those plans in concrete terms

Thus, the Holy Spirit is the "effector" of God's plans in our daily lives. He was behind Jesus's birth and later "filled" Him and guided His actions so that Jesus fulfilled His ministry, all the way to the sacrifice on the cross. The same Spirit filled the believers on the day of Pentecost, empowering them to spread the gospel, remain in communion with God, and become His ambassadors. The same Spirit conveys to us today what in Greek the Bible calls *zoe*, meaning the absolute fullness of life—essential, moral, and eternal—belongs to God. The people who have *zoe* at their disposal will not experience the tribulation of human existence in the same way as those trying to live outside God's realm.

A DIVINE PRINCIPLE

Zoe, this divine principle of life, is often compared
in the Bible to water that spreads throughout barren
places and brings it blessing. For example, in a vision
the prophet Ezekiel described a gushing river flowing
in the valley to the Dead Sea. The prophet told of being
accompanied by a man who showed him God's sanc-
tuary and the river that slips out of it: "He said to me,
'Son of man, have you seen this?' Then he brought me
and caused me to return to the brink of the river. When
I had returned I saw on the bank of the river very many
trees on the one side and on the other. Then he said
to me, 'This water flows toward the eastern region and
goes down into the valley, and enters the sea. When it
flows into the sea, the water will become fresh. Every
living creature that swarms, wherever the rivers go, will
live. And there shall be a very great multitude of fish,
because these waters shall come there and the others
become fresh. Thus everything shall live wherever the
river comes" (Ezek. 47:6–9).

Jeremiah, the prophet who remained faithful as
God's spokesman despite being ignored and eventually
persecuted and killed for his words, also described how
those who are faithful are like trees planted by water:
"Thus says the LORD: Cursed is the man who trusts in
man and makes flesh his strength, and whose heart
departs from the LORD. For he will be like a bush in
the desert and will not see when good comes, but will
inhabit the parched places in the wilderness, in a salt
land and not inhabited. Blessed is the man who trusts

in the LORD, and whose hope is the LORD. For he shall
be as a tree planted by the waters, and that spreads
out its roots by the river, and shall not fear when heat
comes, but its leaf shall be green, and it shall not be
anxious in the year of drought, neither shall cease
from yielding fruit" (Jer. 17:5–8).

Then there is Prophet Isaiah who used a water meta-
phor in alluding to times to come: "Therefore with joy
you shall draw water out of the wells of salvation. In
that day you shall say: Praise the LORD, call upon His
name, declare His deeds among the peoples, make them
remember that His name is exalted" (Isa. 12:3–4). Such
imagery, creating pictures of water to which the tree's
roots extend to draw what allows it to resist the heat and
drought, is a vivid example of *zoe*. This is the life that
God proposes for us to share and through which we are
called to bear fruit. This is God's third objective.

WATER OF LIFE

The prophetic words I just reviewed, and others, point
toward a moment of history where this living water
will be available to all. This moment of history is
indeed about the advent of Jesus Christ. Salvation in
Christ has a direct relationship with this life of God
and makes it accessible to everyone. The realization of
this truth appears in the gospel of John, when Jesus
encountered the Samaritan woman. After describing
living water, He told her, "Everyone who drinks of
this water will thirst again, but whoever drinks of the
water that I shall give him will never thirst. Indeed, the

water that I shall give him will become in him a well of water springing up into eternal life" (John 4:13–14). Jesus used the same water imagery as the prophets to explain the nature and regenerative power of the life available in Him.

Jesus is the door that opens unto God, which is why He told His disciples that He is the way, the truth, and the life. This affirmation leaves no room for ambiguity. No one can go to the Father except through Him! This radical departure from religious tradition also fueled the witness of the Apostle Paul, who in talking about Jesus fearlessly declared to the Jewish leaders (the power brokers of their day), " There is no salvation in any other, for there is no other name under heaven given among men by which we must be saved" (Acts 4:12).

To get to know God is first to know Jesus, and then to receive the Holy Spirit through Him. I am taken with the striking portrait Evangelicals offer of Him, far from traditional, preconceived religious notions. I love the image of the God who lowers Himself to join us weak, flawed human beings in our desperate condition. This is the God who rises up against a legalistic and religious approach to spirituality. The God who gives to us a look at the essentials of life. A generous God, who offers Himself to mankind completely and in dimensions of love most people cannot imagine. The God who frees us from ourselves and the curses to which far too many people have chained themselves. The God who restores our integrity, here and now and for the life to come. Not to inflict rigid lessons of morality on us, but to deliver us and protect us from ourselves!

CHAPTER 11

BEING SPIRITUALLY ACTIVE

Now, brothers, I declare to you the gospel which I preached to you, which you have received, and in which you stand. Through it you are saved, if you keep in memory what I preached to you, unless you have believed in vain. For I delivered to you first of all that which I also received: how Christ died for our sins according to the Scriptures, was buried, rose again the third day according to the Scriptures, and was seen by Cephas, and then by the twelve. Then He was seen by over five hundred brothers at once, of whom the greater part remain to this present time, though some have passed away.

—1 CORINTHIANS 15:1-6

T HE STUDIES I have reviewed thus far reveal that spirituality only offers health benefits when it is put into practice. It does not consist simply of believing; active participation with a local community and engagement with their beliefs is of crucial importance. This is worthwhile highlighting in an era when a growing number of Christians apparently settle for a kind of Church 2.0, with their engagement consisting of a menu of online teachings and videos, or watching cable or satellite programming. While there may be value in cyberspace exchanges, such remote engagement flies in the face of scriptural teaching: "And let us consider how to spur one another to love and to good works. Let us *not forsake the assembling of ourselves together*, as is the manner of some, but let us exhort one another, especially as you see the Day approaching" (Heb. 10:24–25, emphasis added).

In 2011 the respected Barna Group—a widely known and respected demographer of religious trends— released a study of American spiritual life over the previous two decades. Among the major changes it showed were decreases in regular Sunday school and church attendance, Bible reading, and volunteer work. Weekly participation in religious services registered a decline of 9 percent, while the numbers of people skipping church entirely rose by 13 percent. Daily Bible reading declined by 5 percent, leaving only 40 percent who still read the Bible outside of church. Meanwhile volunteer participation in church programs dropped 8 percent, with an average of only one in five adults devoting a part of their time to church activities.[1]

Subsequent surveys have revealed increases in those who don't identify with any church or spiritual community. This is a sad development in light of scientific research that shows how participation in a Christian community is essential for spiritual development and flourishing, and psychological stability. In addition, the purely social aspects of churches and other community-based organizations help people avoid isolation and obtain support in times of calamity or distress. To be involved in a church community enhances spiritual discernment and develops one's Christian character, faith, and sense of responsibility. Rather than getting wrapped up in self, those who experience such growth are capable of turning their attentions and concerns toward others.

The local church also offers the kind of environment where one can move from theory to practice. This helps people respond to the exhortation of the Apostle James, who wrote that we should be "doers of the word and not hearers only, deceiving yourselves. For if anyone is a hearer of the word and not a doer, he is like a man viewing his natural face in a mirror (James 1:22–23).

DEFINING "CHURCH"

A wide variety of Christian churches exist, as do teachings and modes of operation. This spurred respected theologian and professor Wayne Grudem to reflect on what constitutes a church and why these bodies are necessary. In his 1994 book, *Systematic Theology: An Introduction to Biblical Doctrine*, Grudem noted that a group of persons labeling themselves "Christians" could depart so broadly from essential biblical teachings that they could reach the point that their meetings no longer fit the definition of a church.

Grudem wrote that an authentic church should feature certain essentials: "The Lutheran statement of faith, which is called the Augsburg Confession (1530), defined the church as 'the congregation of saints in which the gospel is rightly taught and the sacraments administered alongside the rules.' Similarly, John Calvin said, 'Wherever we see the Word of God purely preached and heard, and the sacraments administered according to Christ's institution, there, it is not to be doubted, a church of God exists.'... Certainly, if the Word of God is not being preached, but simply false doctrines or doctrines of men, then there is no true church."[2]

Besides the preaching and teaching of the Word of God, the administration of the sacraments of baptism and Holy Communion represent a church's other distinctive marks. Through baptism we are admitted to the church, and through Communion one continues to demonstrate one's affiliation with it. For Grudem, that settles it: "Groups who do not administer baptism and the Lord's Supper signify that they are not intending to function as a church.... Even a neighborhood Bible study meeting in a home can have the true teaching and hearing of the Word without becoming a church. But if a local Bible study began baptizing its own new converts and regularly participating in the Lord's Supper, these things would signify *an intention to function as a church* and it would be difficult to say why it should not be considered a church in itself."[3]

It is interesting to note that the New Testament does not offer a particular model for the local church.

This means Christian groups can structure themselves in their own way, provided they respect the New Testament's values and teachings. As an organized human group, no perfect or ideal church exists. On the other hand, criteria exist to differentiate a good church—namely, where believers can be enriched and blossom spiritually—from a dangerous group where sufferings (psychological, spiritual, and even physical) are present. My experience and church history bring me to offer three essentials that should characterize the life of a church: leadership or government, teaching, and mission.

THE FIRST ESSENTIAL: GOVERNMENT

The New Testament likens a Christian leader to a shepherd. This picture presupposes on his or her part a caring attitude concerning those who follow, who are likened to sheep. While such agrarian imagery may seem outdated in a technological age, it was quite compelling in first-century culture, where pastoralism occupied a significant place. By comparing Himself to a shepherd, Jesus established a standard for all leaders: "I am the good shepherd. The good shepherd lays down His life for the sheep....I know My sheep and am known by My own" (John 10:11, 14). In this same passage Jesus warned against the opposite, the mercenaries He called "hired hands" (the King James Version translates this as "hirelings"). Hirelings don't care about the sheep; they care only about their own image or salary and benefits. Earlier in the Gospels Christ warned His followers to be wary of another type of phony leader:

"Beware of false prophets who come to you in sheep's clothing, but inwardly they are ravenous wolves. You will know them by their fruit. Do men gather grapes from thorns, or figs from thistles? Even so, every good tree bears good fruit. But a corrupt tree bears evil fruit" (Matt. 7:15–17).

In spite of such admonitions determining whether a particular leader is a good shepherd or a mercenary, or a true prophet or ravenous wolf, isn't necessarily simple. Fortunately in the church there exist a great many shepherds who give their lives for their sheep. Still, any group must know how to recognize the mercenaries and ravenous wolves who, at best, do not concern themselves with sheep. At worst, they look to feed off of them! I have crossed paths with some of these wolves, who systematically leave traumatized people in their wake. The mercenary, typically a specialist in spiritual abuse, creates a toxic atmosphere. Thus, it is of prime importance to learn to spot negative signals that help discern deviant behaviors.

Harmful consequences are much more likely to occur if the community's government revolves around a small number of individuals. The risk is particularly present among independent groups who are often guided by an individual or a couple (often founders of the community) who in practical terms answer only to themselves. Experience has shown me the mere existence of a council or governing board around the senior person is no guarantee of shared leadership. If the person in charge is authoritarian and manipulative, the leader will know how to surround himself or herself with a team that rubber stamps decisions and, in the case of misconduct, are unable to take a critical look at the leader's methods and schemes.

Church or not, all groups can pose a danger for individuals when manipulative techniques guarantee adherence from its members. Unfortunately this sort of danger is not specific to independent sects. Manipulation and coercion can exist in well-established denominations or churches. Even a church established on sound premises can—over the years— veer toward a sectarian kind of operation, where the person at the top makes all the decisions.

For many years researchers have identified mental manipulation as a tool of coercion. For example, during the Korean War in the early 1950s, after a period of incarceration American prisoners declared their allegiance to the Chinese Communist Party. The Communist regime developed a program of reshaping thought and employed it in universities, educational programs, and Chinese prisons. American psychiatrist and professor Robert Jay Lifton conducted a series of interviews with prisoners and refugees who fled from the Communist regime. In 1961 he released the first edition of *Thought Reform and the Psychology of Totalism: A Study of "Brainwashing" in China* (a book reprinted by the University of North Carolina Press in 1989). Lifton's landmark study defined the methods that lead to mental control. The author outlined eight primary tools that can change individuals' opinion against their will. They can be applied to any social group—unfortunately including churches.

Mental control

Control of the individual's environment

This first technique is to control the person's environment and relationships with the outside world evolve. This can include:

- Controlling information accessible to individuals.

- Controlling the thinking of individuals. The person can no longer judge what is right or wrong; the group decides. They dictate what is suitable to think, do, go, what clothing to wear, and more.

- Controlling the privacy of individuals. The person must not hide anything from leaders or other members. All information concerning members' backgrounds, personal history, and daily activities must be handed over to those in charge—and, under certain circumstances—other members.

Controlling the environment can be facilitated through geographical estrangement, with events or internships offered to recruits who are restricted to an isolated zone. This limits the possibility of participants quitting training without advising another member of the group.

Mystical manipulation

These methods can include such things as:

- Persuading the group of the leader's divine insights. Thus, members voluntarily—often without question—accept the leader's demands or dictates. The leader's claims to possess supernatural powers or exceptional knowledge thereby legitimizes him or her in members' eyes.

- Imposing the leader's choices on all members.

Public confession

In a totalitarian group the confession of thoughts or behaviors deemed "impure" or "bad" often must come before the whole group. This has the effect of eliminating intimacy and rendering everyone's life to public inspection, makes it impossible to keep a secret, and reinforces guilt feelings, ones often stemming from the leader's authoritarian influence.

- Demands for an impossible-to-achieve purity—in a totalitarian group the leader defines what is pure or impure. Thus, the world is separated into two rigid categories, with no place for compromise. This vision of the world influences members' choices, decisions, behaviors, and perceptions. In the groups that value this kind

of purity, leaders often use forms of deprivation. This not only destabilizes the individual, it also hastens the abandonment
of his or her defenses. This can affect
natural needs for sleep, food, or adequate
rest. Among cult leaders' favorite tools
are sports sessions or exercises aimed at
purifying the body, or by prayer sessions
that sometimes last for hours.

These types of groups usually define
purity as a state to achieve. In this sense
all actions taken in the name of purity, or
the fight against impurities, are justified
and even perceived as moral. The leader
encourages members to be vigilant about
the behaviors of others the leader deems
impure. Members are even encouraged
to "inform" on others. Not only is this
a source of conflict, this rigid ideology
also attempts to create guilt feelings
among participants unable to improve. In
these circumstances the leader is often
the sole arbiter and judges of members'
behavior, attitudes, and condition, with
the authority to humiliate or punish
members.

- The group's omniscience—in a totalitarian group the group's doctrine is presented as the only truth, which members
  must not contest; it is their only frame

of reference. Each person must model his or her choices, decisions, and behavior according to this truth. In such circumstances the leader demands affirmation. This means the leader will mask motives for exercising control by offering such comforts as:

- Security. The individual members no longer doubt the leader has the answers to all of life's troubling questions.
- Peace. Less conflict exists when life is full of absolutes.
- Alleviate the need for critical thinking. Because the truth reigns, the model determines what is good or bad.

Acquisition of a new language

In a totalitarian group leaders substitute new language and terms for the familiar.

Words take on new meaning. This shared language can have the effect of creating unity and similarity between members, and allows members and new initiates to feel they "stand out" from nonmembers. The addition of new words or new meanings behind common terms can further isolate members, since only followers of the group can understand this person's remarks. Thus, followers may struggle to communicate with nonmembers. In extreme examples even communication between members can be stilted. This allows leaders to provide followers with different rules of communication that further govern their interactions.

1. The supremacy of the doctrine over the individual

   In a totalitarian group the group's doctrine dominates over any personal values or beliefs. Individuals *must* adopt the group's life philosophy and mission as their sole reference point in life. Leaders often cast expressions of personal values or opinions as "egocentric" or "unhealthy."

2. An existence under threat

   The group that shares a totalitarian vision of existence divides individuals in the community into two camps: those who share their rigid ideology and all others. In this way the members of sectarian groups either minimize or stop exchanges with nonmembers. The members of a totalitarian group have the conviction that only one true life journey exists: theirs. This concept of reality can lead to feelings of fear among persons who yearn to leave; for them, to live outside the group means death. There have even been extreme examples where members of such groups come to believe that only those who share their truth have the right to exist. This grants them permission to decide the right to life or death over nonmembers, or nonbelievers.

A HEAVY YOKE

In these ways people who participate in the confines of such a group inevitably see their lifestyle modified. Because the group provokes an identity crisis, followers often question their old lifestyle and evaluate it according to the group's values. Gradually the person reacts to the pressures of this new environment by adopting the personality entailed in—and desired by—the group, particularly its authoritarian leader. By adopting new attitudes, expressions, and habits valued by the group, the newcomer loses his or her individuality and becomes a "copy" of other members. These characteristics can be found, in varying degrees, among certain churches or Christian groups where mind control and manipulation reign. These techniques are devious, since they appear deceptively similar to authentic spiritual principles. This requires that people learn and use discernment when deciding whether to affiliate with a particular church or group.

Whatever its style and mission, a church should always reflect the sense with which Jesus taught his disciples: "Take My yoke upon you, and learn from Me. For I am meek and lowly in heart, and you will find rest for your souls. For My yoke is easy, and My burden is light" (Matt. 11:29–30). Church leaders should write this passage in gold letters on their bathroom mirrors, in order to contemplate those words regularly and nurture themselves. A reasoned reading of the Scriptures reveals the preferred mode of management Jesus and the first-century church modeled was that of example. This is what Paul the Apostle urged his followers: "Follow me as I follow Christ" (1 Cor. 11:1).

Given these passages, the church should never be a reflection of secular society, no more than it should be managed as a business. Attachment to the ministry and accomplishment of the mission should never prevail over the respect of individuals and the quality of personal relationships. Jesus made this clear in His teaching on heaven: "You know that the rulers of the Gentiles lord it over them, and those who are great exercise authority over them. It shall not be so among you. Whoever would be great among you, let him serve you, and whoever would be first among you, let him be your slave, even as the Son of Man did not come to be served, but to serve and to give His life as a ransom for many" (Matt. 20:25–28).

THE SECOND ESSENTIAL: TEACHING

The church's history has been marked by the development of particular theological movements, depending on the aspect of the Gospels they accent. Thus, in recent decades we have seen such developments as the Word of Faith Movement, the Prophetic Movement, Prosperity Doctrine, the Theology of Freedom, the New Wine, the Toronto Blessing, and the Covenant Movement—to name just a few. Currently it seems that the topic of grace is trendy and often the source of controversies. Certain Christian communities or religious groups will place an excessive emphasis on the gifts of the Holy Spirit, or praise, or missions, or other concepts.

The semi-exclusive development of a particular doctrine, even if it is biblical, runs the risk of eclipsing the others and creating an imbalance in adherents. Unfortunately an overemphasis on one portion of Bible doctrine can lead to misinterpretation or distortion of its meaning and original purpose. This detracts from the Gospel's multifaceted nature. The Gospel can be compared to a rainbow, juxtaposing the light spectrum's different nuances and producing white light. Because it delivers spiritual nourishment, a church should provide a balanced diet to its members.

Various authors have spotlighted the need for theological balance. In his book *Pour une Foi Réfléchie: Théologie pour tous* (For a thoughtful faith: a theology for all), French author and editor Alain Nisus emphasized the centrality of the Word of God as a basis for the church. Since the Bible is its primary form of spiritual nourishment, the preaching and teaching of God's Word must represent its leading activity, he wrote.

"The Church can show creativity in the way of getting across the message in order for it to be more audible, more relevant to the men and women of today (for example, it can have recourse to art, technology, etc.), but it must not invent its faith nor distort its message by trying too hard to adopt it to the current tastes,"

Nisus said. "It lives off a legacy—to know the teaching of the apostles."[4]

In his 2012 book, *The Explicit Gospel*, best-selling author and pastor Matt Chandler distinguished two approaches that are needed—the gospel on the ground and the gospel in the air. This is two aspects of the same reality. The gospel on the ground concerns the work of the cross in the life of human beings. In other words, salvation on a micro-level. On the other hand, the gospel in the air constitutes a macro-level. Namely, an overall restoration such as what the Apostle Paul envisioned: "We know that the whole creation groans and travails in pain together until now. Not only that, but we also, who have the first fruits of the Spirit, groan within ourselves while eagerly waiting for adoption, the redemption of our bodies" (Rom. 8:22–23).

The redemptive work of Jesus does not limit itself to personal salvation; it culminates with the restoration of creation and reveals the totality of the plan of God, who says: "Look! I am making all things new" (Rev. 21:5). A single gospel with two points of view. Yet both indispensable to grasping the full dimension and impact of the good news. If we minimize or reject either perspective, we take the risk of creating an imbalance that can lead to all sorts of errors.

According to Chandler, if we remain at the micro-level for too long, we will run the risk of missing out on God's big plan. Our faith risks being rationalized, with the gospel reduced to an instrument of personal interest: "If we stay focused on the ground too long, we begin to read the Bible with ourselves at the center.... This is a great way to become prideful and arrogant, to rationalize disobedience to the Great Commission and the Great Commandment"[5]

Conversely Chandler says remaining at the macro-level for too long risks drifting toward religious syncretism. This promotes a salvation without Christ—an ethereal, disincarnate gospel that gradually gets mixed up in ambient culture. In effect, if God will end by restoring all things, why do I need invest in myself, for my own life or that of others? The author says the risk is thus great to neglect the good news's proclamation and content oneself with a purely social approach. Those who rest in the air too long can lose sight of the redemptive work of Christ while trying to answer God's call concerning the weak and defenseless, all in the name of a vaguely deistic approach.

In addition to taking a balanced approach, sound teaching is rooted in a belief in the primacy and accuracy of Scripture, as outlined by Paul in his second letter to Timothy: "All Scripture is inspired by God and is profitable for teaching, for reproof, for correction, and for instruction in righteousness, that the man of God may be complete, thoroughly equipped for every good work" (2 Tim. 3:16–17).

The question of inspiration is of the utmost importance. From it flows the Bible's infallible and unerring character. These two almost synonymous notions express that the biblical message is true and trustworthy and that the original, untranslated biblical manuscripts—down to the smallest detail—contain neither error nor contradiction. The attentive analysis of the biblical text as a whole cannot be considered as limited to certain texts or categories.

So, is the Bible fully or only partially inspired? If we were to deem that the Bible is not entirely the Word of God that means man can—through his powers of deduction and reasoning—ascertain what is inspired and what is not. That is a dangerous position to assume, since it means mankind is inserting self into the place occupied solely by God! Moreover, if the Bible is not entirely inspired by God, where can we find the happy medium? How do we determine what came from Him and what didn't?

To respond to the ongoing reassessments of these fundamental questions, in October of 1978 three hundred Protestant theologians from various back-grounds—such as Anglicans, Lutherans, Reformed, and Baptists—signed the Declaration of Chicago regarding biblical inerrancy. A summary:

> God, who is Himself Truth and speaks truth only, has inspired Holy Scripture in order thereby to reveal himself to lost mankind through Jesus Christ as Creator and Lord, Redeemer, and Judge. Holy Scripture is God's witness to Himself.
>
> Holy Scripture, being God's own Word, written by men prepared and superintended by His Spirit, is of infallible divine authority in all matters upon which it touches: It is to be believed,

as God's instruction, in all that it affirms; obeyed, as God's command, in all that it requires; and embraced, as God's pledge, in all that it promises.

The Holy Spirit, its divine Author, both authenticates it to us by His inward witness and opens our minds to understand the meaning of the Word.

Inspired wholly and verbally by God, Scripture is without error or fault in all its teaching, no less in what it states about God's acts in creation, about the events of world history, and about its own literary origins under God (in such that God has led it), than in its witness to God's salvation in individual lives.

The authority of Scripture is inescapably impaired if this total divine inerrancy is in any way limited or neglected, or if we subjugate it to a conception of truth contrary to the Bible's own: the life of the individual and that of the Church seriously suffer from such lapses.[6]

The controversy on inerrancy is not about a minor detail, but how to approach the Bible in its totality and recognize its inspiration—and thus, its authority regarding matters of faith and theology. It is literally the life of the church. Without it a congregation can suffer in the same way an individual does when he or she loses sight of the importance, and centrality, of biblical doctrine. If we surrender the validity of this point, then all of Christian theology can be called into question.

THE THIRD ESSENTIAL: THE MISSION

The Book of Acts offers a description of the first Christians organized in a community. As Luke records it: "They continued steadfastly in the apostles' teaching and fellowship, in the breaking of bread and in the prayers" (Acts 2:42). The brotherly communion illustrated in this passage is (in the Greek) known as *koinonia*. This word is defined as Christian fellowship, which carries the connotations of close sharing, relationships of closeness and reciprocity, and members' actively engaging with one another.

There is a special quality to this kind of closeness. A church is not merely where we go to learn about the Bible—it's also a place of *koinonia*! Nicky Gumble, vicar of London's Holy Trinity Brompton Church and founder of the well-known Alpha course, addressed this in a 2014 article in the Swiss magazine *Le Christianisme Aujourd'hui* (*Christianity Today*). Titled "Friendship, Pillar of the Church and Strength of Believers," in it Gumble asserted: "People come to church for different reasons, but they stay there for one: friendship. People do not look for a nice church, but a church where they can make friends."[7]

An attentive reading of the Gospels shows that Jesus accorded great importance to brotherly love and moments of sharing with His disciples. After His resurrection, we even see Him having a barbecue on the beach with Peter and his companions. (See John 21:9.) This demonstrates how church is the place where believers can find answers to existential questionings and spiritual needs. It's also where they learn to not only love God, but also their brothers and sisters in Christ: "If anyone says, 'I love God,' and hates his brother, he is a liar. For whoever does not love his brother whom he has seen, how can he love God whom he has not seen? We have this commandment from Him: Whoever loves God must also love his brother" (1 John 4:20–21).

To love and feel loved are fundamental human needs, in the same way we all want to feel useful and valued. The satisfaction of such essentials is one of the keys to psychological stability, which has a favorable impact on our overall health. Despite this reality, today's Western society offers fewer possibilities for fulfilling these legitimate aspirations. Sharing, mutual submission, humility, and forgiveness are often missing from the values promoted in the twenty-first-century world. Yet, throughout this book I have detailed the health benefits derived from practicing these qualities. From purely a psychological point of view, and in spite of evolutionists' claims, it is apparent that God "conceived" us for cooperative sharing and love. Pursuing ongoing competition, quarreling, and egocentrism engenders a permanent stress that eats away at us daily. By contrast, the church should be the place where everyone learns—and applies—these essential biblical values.

CHAPTER 12

FAST AND PRAY

Moreover, when you fast, do not be like the
hypocrites with a sad countenance. For they
disfigure their faces so they may appear to
men to be fasting. Truly I say to you, they have
their reward. But you, when you fast, anoint
your head and wash your face, so that you
will not appear to men to be fasting, but to
your Father who is in secret. And your Father
who sees in secret will reward you openly.

—MATTHEW 6:16–18

THROUGHOUT THE BIBLE fasting and prayer
are mentioned as principal ways of interaction
between man and God.

There are numerous forms of fasting, which don't
always involve foregoing food. Still, this discipline
reminds us that "man shall not live by bread alone"
(Luke 4:4) and that "the kingdom of God does not

mean eating and drinking" (Rom. 14:17). Biblical fasting is one of the possibilities God prescribes to free us from the bounds of human flesh and bring us closer to Him. Such Old Testament prophets as Jeremiah, Joel, and Zechariah emphasized the repentance and humility symbolized by fasting. Jesus brought a new spirit to this observance, which He considered a very personal act. Instead of the show the Pharisees favored, He prescribed it as a voluntary act that should take place secretly, with the goal of freeing the soul from the slavery of the flesh and rendering it more accessible to God's direction.

This teaching showed how, in and of itself, fasting is not a means to please God, a form of self-inflicted punishment for our mistakes, or a suffering to be endured as a penalty for our failures. Christ's suffering on the cross ended any such need. His salvation is a free gift that does not depend on the merits of our hunger or thirst. Instead, the goal of fasting is to help us concentrate on God and things above by freeing us from depending on earthly sources. We fast in order to help control our passions, bring to fruition the salvation God offers, and to orient our minds toward Him.

Fasting's value is not solely spiritual, as shown by numerous scientific studies that demonstrate its health benefits. In addition to regular contributing to good health, it can play a role in healing disease. As long ago as the 1950s Ancel Keys—a professor of hygiene and public health at the University of Minnesota—suspected a correlation between food and cardiovascular diseases. In 1958 he launched the Seven Countries Study to compare diet and the proportion of cardio-vascular diseases in Finland, Italy, Yugoslavia, Greece, the Netherlands, Japan, and the United States.

For many years researchers studied the health of ten thousand men, ages forty to sixty, from these seven nations. It revealed that all causes of mortality were greater in the northern countries than in the southern countries; therefore, life expectancy was greater in the latter. A comparison of cardiovascular diseases showed even more striking results. For example, men in the United States showed a 44 percent mortality rate over time, compared to just 1.4 percent on Crete (Greece's largest island). The rate on Crete is thirty times lower than in the United States! More than forty years after the study ended, the monitored populations showed that Cretans maintain the lifestyle and food intake that favors health and prevents heart disease and others, such as cancer.

One attributes these results to diet, obviously, including much lower consumption of animal fats in southern countries—one of the virtues of the Cretan diet. Yet, at the identical cholesterol rate, the mortality rate was ten to twelve times greater in Finland than in Greece. The genetic characteristics of Cretans are not enough to explain these differences. Anthony Kafatos, head of nutrition at Greece's University Hospital of Heraklion, thinks the Cretans' lifestyle can explain these differences. Not just considerable physical activity, but also their higher consumption of fruits, vegetables, and olive oil, which provide an abundance of antioxidant nutrients.

However, a largely unexplored secret of the Cretans' (and Greeks in general) good health involves their religious practices. Prevalent in the region, the Orthodox religion includes numerous fasting periods throughout the liturgical calendar. While not all complete fasts, in the course of most of them, such foods as meat, fish, eggs, cheese, milk, wine, and oil are forbidden. An Orthodox Christian will observe at least a partial fast for more than two hundred days a year!

LONG-TIME PRACTICE

Scripture encourages fasting. Though often overlooked, particularly in the Western world, Christians are supposed to fast regularly. Complete fasting consists of voluntarily denying oneself of food and drink for a short amount of time (often a day or part of a day). Since the church's beginning, Christians understood fasting to be a state of preparation and spiritual concentration for what was to come (i.e., on the eve of a notable liturgical observance). The fast's physical hunger heightened the spiritual anticipation and seeking of God's direction.

Partial fasting consists of renouncing certain types of foods and drinks pleasing to the palate. In his book, *Le Grand Carême: Ascèse et liturgie dans l'Église orthodoxe* (The great lent: asceticism and liturgy in the Orthodox Church), Father Alexander Schmemann—a notable Orthodox theologian in the twentieth century—talked about how the goal of fasting is to free people from the flesh's "debauched tyranny." He said this happens when the spirit caves in to the body's appetites, which at its root resulted in the tragedy of original sin.

"It is only by a slow and patient effort that man can discover that he does not live only on bread, and restores the preeminence of the spirit in himself," Schmemann also said. "It's necessarily and by its very nature a long, steady effort. The 'time' factor is essential, for it is necessary to have the time to uproot and heal the common and universal disease that men have ended up considering as their normal state. The success of this ascetic fasting depends precisely upon the application of certain fundamental rules whose principal happens to be the uninterruption of fasting, its continuation in time."[1]

Another of the early Desert Fathers, Abba Poemen, recalls: "One Saturday evening, the brothers were eating at the church of the Kellia, and as the porridge was presented to the table, Abba Helladios the Alexandrine began to cry. Abba James said to him: 'Why are you crying, abba?' He answered: 'Because the joy of the soul has come to an end, that is, the joy of the fast, and now begins the satisfaction of the body.'"[2]

SCIENTIFIC STUDIES

However, it isn't just spiritual leaders who discuss the benefits of fasting. To amplify my earlier statement about the benefits of fasting, it is worth noting the lengthy span of such scientific studies on this phenomenon. The wealth of evidence ranges from the doctor

Henry Tanner, who fasted for forty days in New York in 1880, to American biologist Valter Longo's modern studies of how fasting benefits cancerous mice. Among the newer works is a 2011 French TV documentary *Fasting: A New Therapy* by writer and cinematographer Thierry de Lestrade (and Sylvie Gilman). This well-documented investigation examined whether fasting is a simple yet effective method for treating diseases. This question is the subject of debate in conventional medical circles, given entrenched dogma against the idea.

The documentary devoted a segment to the research by Soviet doctors from the 1950s to the 1980s. In a book published in 2013 *Le jeûne, une nouvelle thérapie?* (Fasting, a new therapy?), de Lestrade cited a comment from Dr. Yuri Nikolayev, a Soviet psychiatrist who died in 1988: "What is, in your opinion, the most memorable discovery of our century? Jet planes? Television, the radio? Atomic energy? None of those. In my opinion, the greatest discovery of our time is the ability to physically, mentally and spiritually regenerate by fasting. Through using scientific fasting, one can forget his or her age."[3]

Nikolayev, who before his death served as the leader of the Soviet School of Therapeutic Fasting, had been introduced at a young age to fasting's virtues by his father, Serguei Dimitrievitch Nikolayev. The father maintained a connection with American author Upton Sinclair, whose *The Fasting Cure* originally released in 1911, with updated editions still on the market. Three decades later Yuri became bedridden because of a head trauma. He spent idle time by diving into ancient writings by men who recognized the therapeutic virtues of fasting, as well as Russian researchers with similar views. After founding the Psychiatric Institute of Moscow, Nikolayev tried to integrate fasting into treatments, despite the opposition from authorities. After a rough start, he made progress with some schizophrenic patients. The turning point came when he rescued the son of the Soviet Union's second-highest ranking official.

Although the Soviets then approved considerable studies of fasting, it took a while for Westerners to learn about them. In 1972 the Moscow correspondent for the *Los Angeles Times* wrote about the research at the Psychiatric Institute of Moscow that reviewed the efficacy of treating mental pathologies through fasting. The article spurred international recognition. It prompted visits by an American psychiatrist and biologist, and a 1974 article in *Orthomolecular Psychiatry* titled, "Controlled Fasting Treatment for Schizophrenia." Other articles followed. As summarized by de Lestrade, Russian doctors discovered three primary psychotropic effects from such treatments:

- A stimulating and antidepressive effect during the first week of fasting

- A calming and sedative effect during the second week, including reduced hallucinations

- Accentuation of stimulating and antidepressive effects afterward

Fasting not only seemed to relieve symptoms, it also affected the patients' physical well-being and personality. Unfortunately a lack of funding and pressure from pharmaceutical firms helped curtail these studies. Even then certain Russian practitioners did not hesitate to propose fasting to patients as a complement or alternative to modern pharmaceutical methods.

THERAPEUTIC FASTING

Another major contributor to the field of therapeutic fasting was German doctor Otto Buchinger. Acute rheumatoid arthritis left him 100 percent disabled in 1917. Forced to leave his position as a health officer in the German navy, and beset by despair, he followed a nineteen-day fasting cure in Freiburg at the home of a colleague. The spectacular results exceeded all expectations. Buchinger wrote in his memoirs: "This nineteen-day fast really saved my life. I was weak, thinner, but my joints had become moveable and painless again."[4]

After being cured, Dr. Buchinger dedicated his medical career to using fasting for patient treatment, opening the world's first specialized clinic in Ueberlingen in 1953. After his death in 1966 others saw the light, including Dr. Francoise Wilhemi de Toledo, the wife of Dr. Buchinger's grandson. Author of *The Art of Fasting* (2003) she remains a fervent advocate of this natural method. A recent article in the *London Telegraph* about her work noted, "Fasting, as part of a lifestyle is, she believes, undoubtedly a good thing but her focus is on making it part of the armamentarium available to doctors coping with an epidemic of lifestyle diseases in the West that threaten to cripple healthcare systems. It has been shown to lower blood pressure, reduce excess fat and glucose in the blood, modulate the immune system, increase the effect of the mood and sleep regulating neuro-transmitter serotonin, promote protein repair, boost the growth of 'good' bacteria in the gut and reduce inflammation."[5]

As for Dr. Buchinger, he would no doubt be pleased to discover that, despite obstacles erected by Western medical voices and a lack of research funds, public health authorities (at least in Germany) have awakened to the promise of therapeutic fasting. De Lestrade mentioned how, in early 2000, an entire floor of an annex of the Berlin Charity Hospital was set aside for patients undergoing fasting treatments. A dozen public hospitals followed suit and gradually this practice has become more reputable. To demonstrate their value, they are now reimbursed by German health insurers.

Other, more recent developments have also accented fasting's therapeutic value. Since the late 1980s Valter Longo, the professor from the University of Southern California I mentioned earlier, has studied aging and cellular degeneration. He and his team have conducted numerous studies showing the benefits of caloric restriction and fasting on health and longevity. Among their discoveries was that in cancer cases fasting created a stress that forced normal cells to protect themselves. Not only are cancerous cells more vulnerable and sensitive to treatment, fasting also protects patients from these treatments' often-damaging effects.

In addition, Longo's laboratory studies have demonstrated fasting's protective effects against the effects of aging. Recently he highlighted fasting's positive effects on the immune system, showing how a three-day fast can allow for the immune system's complete regeneration. How? By stimulating stem cells so that they transform themselves into white blood cells. This can benefit both cancer patients and those with a deficient immune system. Longo comments: "Fasting gives the OK for stem cells to go ahead and begin proliferating and rebuild the entire system. And the good news is that the body got rid of the parts of the system that might be damaged or old, the inefficient parts, during the fasting. Now, if you start with a system heavily damaged by chemotherapy or aging, fasting cycles can generate, literally, a new immune system."[6]

This approach goes against the grain of traditional cancer treatment. For years medical practitioners have often sought to overfeed patients in an effort to restore their energy—which appears to be grist for the mill of the cancerous process. Naturally any trend needs careful observations and prudence. More clinical evidence is needed before physicians can recommend fasting. As a further caution, no studies reveal that fasting alone cures. If afflicted with this disease, specialized medical care is still essential!

OTHER PROTECTION

Other studies show protection from the effects of cerebral aging. Researchers from the National Institute on Aging in Baltimore discovered that fasting one or two days a week can protect against Alzheimer's or Parkinson's disease. Researchers have also shown that a five-thousand-calorie decrease of one's dietary intake for one or two days a week has beneficial effects on the brain.[7]

Other studies highlight protective and preventative effects against diabetes and cardiovascular diseases. Despite such encouraging results, medical research on fasting's benefits runs into a major, aforementioned problem: funding. The longest-lasting and costliest clinical studies needed for the authorization of new treatments are largely funded by pharmaceutical companies. Like other "nonindustrial" alternatives, fasting researchers can typically only rely on limited public research funds.

While such information prompts a desire to try fasting, yet—like me—you allow inertia to hold you back, remember the spiritual benefits as well. Depriving the body of caloric intake causes several reactions. With energy input a priority for cellular metabolism, the body immediately mobilizes internal reserves of sugars and in fats (which demonstrates how God provided built-in mechanisms to survive food shortages). During the first twenty-four hours of fasting your body draws on such energy reserves as glycogen, a complex sugar stored in the liver and muscles. After these are exhausted, it stocks up on protein reserves, notably from the muscles. Doctors once thought this meant fasting could be dangerous because of muscle loss, especially in the heart. However, we now know that the body knows how to protect its protein reserves.

After about ten days without food, the body starts using fat storage. Studies of penguins of Antarctica revealed this phase can last for about one hundred days. In the adult male standing five feet, seven inches tall and weighing about 154 pounds, the fat supply is about 33 pounds, which would allow one to go about forty days without food—the length of Christ's fast in the desert (see Matthew 4). To compensate for the lack of glucose, the body creates a substitute via proteins and lipids. Due to this change of feeding method, levels of acidity in the blood increase. The body must learn how to live off these reserves. According to those who fast regularly, the most difficult thing is not the sensations of hunger—which gradually fade—but the acidosis crisis that can cause nausea, headaches, abdominal pains, cramps, and general weakness.

MAKING PREPARATIONS

From a practical point of view, how can one fast safely in order to reap all of the benefits? I have talked with numerous believers who approach this discipline with considerable zeal. Yet they lack sensible caution, exposing themselves to negative side effects. Because fasting embodies a sort of physiological electroshock, anyone planning to fast should prepare for this change in food intake. Beforehand, consult a physician to check overall health and such vital signs as blood pressure, pulse, weight, and body temperature.

One of the effects of a fast is a disruption of your ability to regulate body temperature. This is the very reason one ought to avoid this practice if exposed to either a cold, rigorous climate or excessive heat, which pose difficulties in adapting to climate. This is why, in several religious traditions, extended fasts occur in spring or fall, outside of these extremes.

In addition, don't forget that during a fast your body lives off its own reserves. Moreover, this is not just physical, but also a spiritual practice aimed at guiding your spirit to be more attentive toward God. This is a primary reason you should avoid fasting when facing demanding professional or personal obligations that require time, focus, or emotional energy.

Thus, the most successful and rewarding fast will be a planned fast, especially if it extends over several days. Here are three steps to follow:

A preparatory phase of a few days of progressively reducing food intake. During this time, eliminate animal foods and follow a vegetarian diet.

The fast itself, whether total or partial.

A phase of progressive food reintroduction of two or three days, where one gradually resumes consumption of foods removed during the preparatory phase.

At the start of the fasting phase, you may feel hunger pangs, but they generally fade after the second day. If you prepare as recommended, such symptoms as headaches, nausea, dizziness, and muscular pains are generally fleeting. From the second or third day, they make way for a feeling of lightness—even a kind of euphoria and greater clarity of mind. Forget those who advise skipping water. You should drink more water during a fast. After ending it, progressively reintroduce food to avoid "the rebound effect," which refers to the body quickly storing fat from a rapid increase in caloric intake. This effect is why many fasters see their weight increase over time, similar to the yo-yo effect that follows popular, restrictive slimming diets.

Remember that fasting is not intended to traumatize your delicate biological machine, which is why this practice demands using common sense and wise precautions. Any "beginner" must start off with a day of abstinence, or a few days, before contemplating a longer duration as part of an ongoing lifestyle.

THE PRACTICE OF PRAYER

Dr. Andrew Newberg, whose work I mentioned in chapter 7, has done extensive studies of the effects of prayer and meditation on the human brain. In 2012 on the Science TV channel's *Through the Wormhole*, he explained his method: he injects a harmless radioactive substance into his patient's brain while the patient is in the midst of prayer or meditation. The product moves through the most irrigated zones; these are most active at that moment. In one experiment on a Presbyterian pastor images showed increased activity in the frontal lobes and speech centers—the part of the brain stimulated during a conversation.

This enabled Newberg to establish a parallel with Judeo-Christian tradition, in which prayer leads to a dialogue with God. In studies of Buddhist meditation that involve visualization, he also observed a change or more intense activity in the visual part of their brains. On the other hand, in atheists no noticeable activity occurs in the frontal lobes. This led the doctor to deduce that, for believers, God is as real as the visible, tangible world. Said Newberg: "And thus, this helps us to understand that when they describe it to us, they are truly in the process of experiencing it. In any case, this experience is from a neurological point of view."[8] Other studies at New York's famed Columbia University confirm that regular prayer changes the brain's structure and operations.

While some people treat prayer as routine or a kind of religious obligation, scientists have chronicled a series of benefits stemming from regular prayer. Researchers across the world have discovered that prayer:

- Influences the state of mind and contributes to the reduction of stress—mental, physical, and emotional

- Reduces the risk of depression and anxiety and increases the probability of a positive, optimistic outlook

- Exercises an extremely positive influence on managing mental and emotional disturbances

- Reduces disorders provoked by stress, such as cardiovascular diseases, autoimmune diseases, digestive and neurological pathologies, and certain types of cancer

- Increases feelings of happiness and well-being by increasing dopamine levels

- Modulates the functioning of cerebral zones regulating emotions, and allows for a decrease in ego, which renders the individual more humble and empathetic and less attached to material things

- Reduces recovery time after an operation and contributes to the acceleration of the processes of cicatrization (healing from a wound)

- Strengthens the organism's immune defenses and better enables it to fight diseases, particularly infections

- Exercises numerous benefits on heart function and also increases the speed of recovery after a heart attack or operation

- Because of these benefits, ongoing prayer helps people live better and longer. One study in the 1990s of nearly four thousand elderly people in North Carolina showed that those who prayed or meditated regularly got sick less and lived better and longer than those who did not.[9]

Other studies worldwide report similar health benefits of meditative practices. Many concern meditation derived from Buddhist practices, such as MBSR (Mindfulness Based Stress Reduction), which offers undeniable physical and mental health benefits. Thanks to medical imaging technologies, it is possible to state that—in only a few days—regular meditative practice modifies brain structure and operations.

RICH IN MEDITATION

Yet, meditation is not exclusive to Buddhism. Stretching back to the origin of its sacred texts, Christianity is rich in meditative and contemplative culture. Type "contemplate" or "meditate" into a biblical search engine and an incalculable number of verses instantly appear. Psalms written by David are just one example:

> O God, You are my God; early will I seek You; my soul thirsts for You, my flesh faints for You, in a dry and thirsty land with no water. I have seen You in the sanctuary, to see Your power and Your glory.... My soul will be satisfied as with marrow and fatness, and my mouth will praise You with

joyful lips. When I remember You on my bed, and meditate on You in the night watches.

—PSALM 63:1–6

I sought the Lord, and He answered me, and delivered me from all my fears. They looked to Him and became radiant, and their faces are not ashamed.

—PSALM 34:4–5

The author of Psalm 46 gives God Himself the floor when He declares in verse 10: "Be still and know that I am God!"

The Apostle Paul urges the same kind of stillness in his writings. To be still and allow the nature of God to establish itself in our consciousness is essence of Christian meditation. Putting ourselves on "pause" mode helps us to lift our gaze above everyday life and circumstances. As Paul says:

If you then were raised with Christ, desire those things which are above, where Christ sits at the right hand of God. Set your affection on things above, not on things on earth. For you are dead, and your life is hidden with Christ in God.

—COLOSSIANS 3:1–3

We do not look at the things which are seen, but at the things which are not seen. For the things which are seen are temporal, but the things which are not seen are eternal.

—2 CORINTHIANS 4:18

Numerous prayers exist for all sorts of circumstances. Referring to scientific research, it appears that meditative forms are the most beneficial for health. A prayer of the heart is still practiced by Christians in the Orient and Orthodox traditions. They call on Jesus (or *hesychia*—from the Greek ἡσυχασμός, *hesychasmos*, from ἡσυχία, *hesychia*, meaning immobility, rest, calm, silence). While the form and words may vary, such prayers are always simple and short so they can be repeated without distraction. Among them are:

- In the Greek, *"Kyrie Eleison."*

- According to an ancient tradition that remains widespread: "Lord, have mercy."

- The Orthodox Church prefers: "Lord, have mercy upon us."

Other examples of short prayers appear in the Gospels, such as Peter's effective cry as he sinks in the water: "Lord, save me!" (Matt. 14:30). In any case it's about a simple prayer that fits multiple activities and can be offered internally, without interruption. Such prayers offer a simplicity that allows the speaker to concentrate on God's presence. In this sense the prayer of Jesus is described not as an end, but as a means to a path toward pure prayer, without words, in a heart-to-heart exchange.

Rachel Goettman, the codirector of Bethanie, a center for spiritual encounters in eastern France, once wrote in the center's quarterly journal, *Le Chemin*, that

what leads to an experience is not a prayer spoken by
Jesus, nor of a prayer to Jesus (even though prayer is
addressed to Him), but an invocation that makes the
difference. In such cases every word delivered is an
experience and can only live in the Holy Spirit.

"Let us say straight away that Jesus's Prayer is a path
within the hesychaste prayer, this 'method' of meditation or oration that wants, in the silence and peace
of the heart, to meet the living God in the Trinitarian
life," she wrote. "The hesychaste is the one that creates
a 'return into oneself,' which looks to silence itself so
that God may speak to Him, knowing well that such
an intent is not only met through a single teaching. It's
a question of spiritual experience, a meeting. *Hesychia*
is to remain before God in incessant prayer; that the
memory of Jesus should unite itself with your breathing
and you will know the value of *hesychia*. If practicing
hesychia is to draw closer to God, how can we then
know Him if He does not manifest Himself in us, if
He does not make Himself known to us down to His
name? Otherwise God would not be the living God.

"It's in this approach to God, in this thirst for His
manifestation, that Jesus's prayer is born from oriental
Christian monasticism: Lord Jesus Christ, Son of God,
have pity on me, the sinner. It unites the soul with the
Lord Jesus Christ, and He is the only door to communion with God, which is the goal of every meeting
(Theophane the Recluse). We do not learn Jesus's prayer,
we enter into the experience...."[10]

Relaxation Response

In this sense, from a neurobiological point of view, *hesychia* would act in the same way as the Buddhist mantras studied extensively by neurobiologists. According to these Eastern traditions, the mantra is a condensed formula of one or a series of syllables. It is repeated numerous times following a certain rhythm, with the objective of channeling the mental discursive. These virtues, combined with the reciter's intention and concentration, appear beneficial from a neurobiological perspective. Thus, the mantra is a support for meditation. The goal of this practice can be for physical or spiritual benefit.

It is reminiscent of what Herbert Benson described in his well-known 1975 reference work, *The Relaxation Response*, issued in an updated and expanded edition in 2001. From a health point of view, Benson's work indicates two ingredients are necessary in triggering this beneficial response:

- The repetition, silent or aloud, of a phrase, word, or sound

- A passive attitude, with no concern for the quality of performance and focusing on a thought while avoiding the intrusion of parasitic ideas

John Raleigh Mott (along with Emily Greene Balch) received the Nobel Peace Prize in 1946 for his involvement in the creation of the YMCA and World Student

Christian Federation, which worked to promote world peace. As part of his work, Mott composed a short message titled *The Morning Watch*, which became a classic and is used by the YMCA and such groups as Alcoholics Anonymous. Among excerpts from this seminal work that discuss the need for starting the day in prayer and meditation:

> There is no more encouraging fact in the life of the Church at the present time than the increase in the number of Christians who observe the morning watch. By the observance of the morning watch is commonly meant the spending of at least the first half-hour of every day alone with God in personal devotional Bible study and prayer...
>
> After praying and during Bible study, it is well to pause and listen to what the Lord shall say. Too often we fill up the devotional hour with our own thoughts and prayers and leave no still place for listening...After we shut out the voices of the world turmoil, after we banish the suggestions of the tempter, after we cease to listen to the thoughts about the morrow, after we silence the sound of our own cares, questions and prayers then we hear that still, small voice which His true followers always know.[11]

Mott's comments have deep roots, going back to first-century monasticism and the creation of the *"Lectio divina."* The term refers to a meditative and prayerful reading of the Word of God. It entails careful attention and listening. Saint Ambrose, a bishop of Milan and influential leader of the fourth century, once said that this attention should be such that the whole person stretches toward listening to the Word.

Enzo Bianchi, the Catholic layman who established Italy's ecumenical Monastic Community of Bose in 1965, wrote in *Praying the Word: An Introduction to Lectio Divina*, that if our attention is total and abandon complete, then full adhesion with God is easy.

"Thus, one ought to search in reading, that is to say meditate upon it in an endeavor to understand the meaning there, thanks to the illumination of the Holy Spirit," he wrote. "But the most important part of this process is the rumination of the Word, to return incessantly to the text, by finding the central theme, by repeating the words and engraving them deeply onto one's heart. To ponder the Word is to spiritually consume the Gospel, and in that way the Gospel becomes food and drink in this contemplative continuation of reflection."[12]

To conclude this chapter, I will give the floor to Rob Moll. A journalist and writer, he is the author of *What Your Body Knows About God*. In an interview with the journal *Christianity Today*, he made some particularly relevant observations about our relationship with God:

> The human body is an extraordinary creation of God, yet Scripture also tells us how ordinary it is, made of simple dust. We live this paradox, that we are both dust and imago Dei. How much more was Jesus, the incarnated God? I wonder

if any of us, if we had been able to meet Jesus, would have thought that he was God. God was so fully incarnated that we might have scoffed at him or walked by without a second glance....

We remember that God works not only in sweeping miraculous ways, but also in our bodies through the DNA, cells, and biological structures that he's created. It may be hard to look at a part of our make up and say, "Oh, that part's God." Yet even the seemingly mundane functions of the body can evoke wonder when we consider them in light of the Creator. In incarnation, the ordinary and the extraordinary are woven seamlessly together. This is true of the person of Jesus; it's true of us as well.[13]

Writing this book has been a very long process. I spent a lot of time examining Scripture and reviewing a huge amount of scientific literature, searching for evidence of a link between faith and health. What I discovered far exceeded my expectations. Not only does this faith link exist—and there is plenty of evidence to prove it—but this search also cast a new light on the Word of God itself! What appeared as only strict orders from the Lord are actually words of wisdom and love for our own preservation and protection. I hope that, like me, you enjoyed this journey and that you can recognize the God of the Bible is truly One we can trust for a balanced and healthy life.

Beloved, I pray that in all respects you may prosper and be in good health, just as your soul prospers.

—3 JOHN 2, NAS

NOTES

INTRODUCTION

1. Larry Dossey, *Healing Words* (New York: HarperCollins, 1994).

CHAPTER 1:
FAITH AND HEALING: A CONTINUOUS TRADITION

1. William DeArtega, *Quenching the Spirit* (Lake Mary, FL: Creation House, 1992), 83.

2. Guy Jalbert, *"Jésus, le divin médecin* (Jesus, the divine physician)" in *Selon Sa Parole* (According to His Word) 26, no. 5 (November/December 2000).

3. Jean-Claude Larchet, *Thérapeutique des maladies spirituelles* (Nice, France: L'Ancre, 1991), 322.

4. Thomas W. Merrill, "Masters and Possessors of Nature," *New Atlantis*, accessed October 12, 2015, http://www.thenew atlantis.com/publications/masters-and-possessors-of-nature.

5. Thierry Janssen, *La Maladie a-t-elle un sens?* (Paris, France: Fayard, 2008), 28.

6. Burr Eichelmann, "Religion, Spirituality, and Medicine," *American Journal of Psychiatry*, December 12, 2007, accessed October 12, 2015, http://ajp.psychiatryonline.org/toc/ajp/164/12.

7. Dale Matthews, *The Faith Factor* (New York: Penguin Books, 1999), 5.

CHAPTER 2:
HOW FAITH REDUCES STRESS

1. K. I. Pargament et al., "God Help Me: (I): Religious Coping Efforts as Predictors of the Outcomes to Significant

Negative Life Events," *American Journal of Community Psychology* 18, no. 6 (1990): 793–824.

2. Matthews, *The Faith Factor*, 145.

3. "Religion," Gallup Organization, accessed October 27, 2015, http://www.gallup.com/poll/1690/religion.aspx.

CHAPTER 3:
HEALTHY IS THE LORD!

1. Joshua Wolf Shenk, "What Makes Us Happy?", *Atlantic*, June 2009, accessed October 28, 2015, http://www.theatlantic.com/magazine/archive/2009/06/what-makes-us-happy/307439/.

2. George Vaillant, *The Natural History of Alcoholism* (Cambridge, MA: Harvard University Press, 1983), 193.

3. Ibid.

4. Harold G. Koenig et al., "Religious Practices and Alcoholism in a Southern Adult Population," *Hospital and Community Psychiatry* 45 (1994): 225–231.

5. Harold G. Koenig et al., "The Relationship Between Religious Activities and Cigarette Smoking in Older Adults," *Journal of Gerontology* (medical sciences) 53A (1998): M426–M434.

6. Harold G. Koenig, *The Healing Power of Faith* (New York: Simon & Schuster, 1999).

CHAPTER 4:
FAITH AND PSYCHOLOGICAL TROUBLES

1. "Understanding Suicide," Fact Sheet, 2015, Centers for Disease Control and Prevention, accessed October 27, 2015, http://www.cdc.gov/violenceprevention/pdf/suicide_factsheet-a.pdf.

CHAPTER 5:
MIND GAMES

1. Richard O'Connor, *Undoing Perpetual Stress: The Missing Connection Between Depression, Anxiety, and 21st Century Illness* (New York: Berkley Books, 2005), 1.

2. Janice K. Kiecolt-Glaser, "Slowing of Wound Healing by Psychological Stress," *Lancet* 346, no. 8984, 1194–1196.

3. Phillip T. Marucha, Janice K. Kiecolt-Glaser, and Mehrdad Favagehi, "Mucosal Wound Healing Is Impaired by Examination Stress," *Psychosomatic Medicine* 60, no 4, accessed October 16, 2015, https://interferon.osumc.edu/KG%20 Publications%20(pdf)/118.pdf.

4. Berton Kaplan, "Social Health and the Forgiving Heart: The Type B Story," *Journal of Behavorial Medicine* 15, no. 1 (February 1992): 3–14), accessed October 28, 2015, http://link .springer.com/article/10.1007%2FBF00848374.

CHAPTER 6:
THE SHIELD OF FAITH

1. Jerf Wai-keung Yeung and Yuk-chung Chan, "The Positive Effects of Religiousness on Mental Health in Physically Vulnerable Populations," *International Journal of Psychosocial Rehabilitation* 11, no. 2 (2007): 37–52.

2. Ian Brisette, Michael F. Scheier, and Charles S. Carver, "The Role of Optimism in Social Network Development, Coping, and Psychological Adjustment During a Life Transition," *Journal of Personality and Social Psychology* 82, no. 1 (2002): 102–111, accessed October 19 2015, http://psycnet.apa .org/journals/psp/82/1/102/.

3. N. A. Peterson and J. Hughey, "Social Cohesion and Intrapersonal Empowerment: Gender as Moderator," Health Education Research 19, no. 5 (2004): 533–542; J. P. Hewitt, *Self and Society: A Symbolic Interactionist Social Psychology* (Boston, MA: Allyn & Bacon, 1991) as cited in "The Positive Effects of Religiousness on Mental Health in Physically Vulnerable Populations."

4. James W. Jones, "Religion, Health and the Psychology of Religion," *Journal of Religion and Health* 43, no. 4 (December 2004): 317–328, accessed October 30, 2015, http://link.springer .com/article/10.1007%2Fs10943-004-4299-3.

CHAPTER 7:
WIRED FOR GOD!

1. Corinne Bensimon, "Homme-Singe, Mode d'Emploi (Man vs ape, user manual)," *Libération* 29 (September 1998).

2. Andrew Newberg and Mark Roberts Waldman, *How God Changes Your Brain* (New York: Ballantine Books, 2009), 4–7.

3. Yakir Kaufman et al., "Cognitive Decline in Alzheimer Disease," *Neurology* 68, no. 18 (May 1, 2007): 1509–1514.

4. Mihály Csíkszentmihályi, *Flow: The Psychology of Optimal Experience* (New York: Harper & Row, 1990), 3.

5. Newberg and Waldman, *How God Changes Your Brain*, 38.

6. Ibid., 33.

7. Mario Beauregard and Denyse O'Leary, *The Spiritual Brain* (San Francisco, CA: HarperOne, 2007), 29–30.

8. Ibid., 28–29, 34.

9. Ibid.

CHAPTER 8:
NOT ANY FAITH WILL DO

1. Richard Beck and C. Dewayne Miller, "Religiosity and Agency and Communion: Their Relationship to Religious Judgmentalism," *Journal of Psychology: Interdisciplinary and Applied* 134, no. 3 (2000); S. D. Bailey, "Religious Orientation and the Expression of Racial Prejudice Among Graduate Students in the Field of Psychology," *Dissertation Abstracts International-B* 61 (2000): 3048; C. E. Cannon, "The Influence of Religious Orientation and White Racial Identity on Expressions of Prejudice," *Dissertation Abstracts International-B* 62, (2001): 598; R. T. Lundblad, "Social, Religious, and Personal Contributors to Prejudice," *Dissertation Abstracts International-B* 63 (2002): 589.

2. C. Daniel Batson, Patricia Schoenrade, and W. Larry Ventis, *Religion and the Individual: A Social-Psychological Perspective* (Oxford, England: Oxford University Press, 1993).

3. C. Daniel Batson et al., "'And Who Is My Neighbor?' Quest Religion as a Source of Universal Compassion," *Journal for the Scientific Study of Religion* 40, (2001): 39–50.

4. Dustin A. Pardini et al., "Religious Faith and Spirituality in Substance Abuse Recovery: Determining the Mental Health Benefits," *Journal of Substance Abuse Treatment* 19, no. 4 (December 2000): 347–354, accessed October 20, 2015, http://www.ncbi.nlm.nih.gov/pubmed/11166499.

5. Sigmund Freud, *Civilization and Its Discontents* (New York: W. W. Norton & Co., 1927), 12.

6. Albert Ellis, *The Case Against Religion* (Austin, TX: American Atheist Press), 55.

7. Urs Winter et al., "The Psychological Outcome of Religious Coping With Stressful Life Events in a Swiss Sample of Church Attendees," *Psychotherapy and Psychosomatics* 78 (2009): 240–244.

8. Paul Copan, *Is God a Moral Monster?* (Grand Rapids, MI: Baker Books, 2011), 55.

9. Samuel Pfeifer, *La Foi est-elle un Facteur de Déséquilibre?* (Is faith a factor of imbalance?).

10. J. Lee Grady, *The Holy Spirit Is Not for Sale* (Grand Rapids, MI: Chosen Books, 2010), 59.

11. Bette L. Bottoms et al., "In the Name of God: A Profile of Religion-Related Child Abuse," *Journal of Social Issues* 51, 2 (1995): 85–111, accessed October 20, 2015, http://online library.wiley.com/doi/10.1111/j.1540-4560.1995.tb01325.x /abstract.

CHAPTER 9:
THE VIRTUES OF CHRISTIAN CHARACTER

1. Arthur Brooks, *Gross National Happiness* (New York: Basic Books, 2008), 175.

2. Jill Neimark, "The Good Life," *Spirituality & Health*, May/June 2007, 14, accessed October 20, 2015, http://www .whygoodthingshappen.com/downloadable/jill_neimark_open _mind.pdf.

3. Stephen Post and Jill Weimark, *When Good Things Happen to Good People* (New York: Broadway Books, 2007), xiii.

4. Piero Ferrucci, *The Power of Kindness: The Unexpected Benefits of Leading a Compassionate Life*, (New York: Tarcher, 2006), 4.

5. Ibid., 4.

6. Robert Emmons, *Thanks!* (Boston, MA: Houghton Mifflin Harcourt, 2007), 15, 17.

7. Ibid., 18.

8. See "Researching the Process Model of Forgiveness Within Psychological Interventions" by Robert D. Enright and Catherine T. Coyle in Everett L. Worthington Jr., *Dimensions of Forgiveness: Psychological Research and Theological Perspectives* (Radnor, PA: Templeton Foundation Press, 1998), 139–161.

9. A. Macaskill, J. Maltby, and L. Day, "Failure to Forgive Self and Others: A Replication and Extension of the Relationship Between Forgiveness, Personality, Social Desirability and General Health," *Personality and Individual Differences* 181 (2001): 1–6.

CHAPTER II:
BEING SPIRITUALLY ACTIVE

1. "Barna Examines Trends in 14 Religious Factors Over 20 Years (1991 to 2011)," The Barna Group, July 25, 2011, accessed October 21, 2015, https://www.barna.org/barna-update/faith -spirituality/504-barna-examines-trends-in-14-religious-factors -over-20-years-1991-to-2011#.VdHfxJd1z3U.

2. Wayne Grudem, *Systematic Theology: An Introduction to Biblical Doctrine* (Grand Rapids, MI: Zondervan, 1994), 865.

3. Ibid., 866.

4. Alain Nisus, *Pour une foi réfléchie, théologie pour tous* (Lausanne, Switzerland: La Maison de la Bible, 2011), 588.

5. Matt Chandler, *The Explicit Gospel* (Wheaton, IL: Crossway Books, 2012), 188.

6. "The Chicago Statement on Biblical Inerrancy," The Evangelical Theological Society, October 1978, accessed October 21, 2015, http://www.etsjets.org/files/documents /Chicago_Statement.pdf.

7. Nicky Gumble, "Friendship, Pillar of the Church and Strength of Believers," *Christianisme Aujourd'hui*, June 2014.

CHAPTER 12:
FAST AND PRAY

1. Alexander Schmemann et al., "The Fast as Spiritual Warfare," accessed October 30, 2015, http://www.pages orthodoxes.net/metanoia/jeuner.htm.

2. "Abba Poemen," *Apophthegmata Patrum* (Sayings of the Desert Fathers) in William Harmless in *Desert Christians: An Introduction to the Literature of Early Monasticism*, (Oxford, England: Oxford University Press, 2004), 206–211.

3. Thierry de Lestrade, *Le jeûne, une nouvelle thérapie?* (Fasting, a new therapy?) (Paris: La Découverte, 2013), 154.

4. Otto Buchinger *About Fasting*, trans. Geoffrey Dudley (n.p.: Thorsons Publishers, 1961).

5. Liz Hunt, "Is Fasting the Key to Weight Loss, Good Health, Youthful Vitality and Longevity?", *London Telegraph*, April 13, 2015, accessed October 30, 2015, http://www.telegraph .co.uk/lifestyle/wellbeing/11527318/Is-fasting-the-key-to-weight -loss-good-health-youthful-vitality-and-longevity.html.

6. Sarah Knapton, "Fasting for Three Days Renews Entire Immune System, Protects Cancer Patients, 'Remarkable' New Study Finds," *Daily Telegraph*, June 5, 2014, accessed October 30, 2015, http://news.nationalpost.com/health/fasting-for -three-days-renews-entire-immune-system-protects-cancer -patients-remarkable-new-study-finds.

7. Martin Bronwen, Mark Pattson, and Stuart Maudsley, "Caloric Restriction and Intermittent Fasting: Two Potential Diets for Successful Brain Aging," *Ageing Research Reviews* 5, no. 3 (August 2006): 332–353, accessed October 30, 2015, http://www.ncbi.nlm.nih.gov/pmc/articles/PMC2622429/.

8. To view the clip "Andrew Newberg: Is the Human Brain Hardwired for God?" visit https://www.youtube.com/watch ?v=uxREBlWvxfk; Johnabi Barooah, "Study Shows How Prayer, Meditation Affect Brain Activity" *Huffington Post*, October 18, 2012, accessed December 9, 2015, http://www.huffingtonpost .com/2012/10/18/how-does-prayer-meditation-affect-brain -activity_n_1974621.html; Richard Schiffman, "Why People Who Pray Are Healthier Than Those Who Don't" *Huffington Post*, January 18, 2012, accessed December 9, 2015, http://www .huffingtonpost.com/richard-schiffman/why-people-who-pray -are-heathier_b_1197313.html.

9. Hughes M. Helm et al., "Does Private Religious Activity Prolong Survival? A Six-Year Follow-Up Study of 3,851 Older Adults," *Journals of Gerontology*, November 15, 1999, accessed October 30, 2015, http://biomedgerontology.oxfordjournals .org/content/55/7/M400.full.

10. Rachel Goettman, "Revue," *Le Chemin*, no. 21, 1993.

11. John Raleigh Mott, *The Morning Watch* (Geneva, Switzerland: International Young Men's Christian Association, 1898), 1, 4.

12. Enzo Bianchi, *Praying the Word* (Collegeville, MN: Cistercian Publications, 1998), 64.

13. Amy Julia Becker, "The Great Congruence of Science and Faith," *Christianity Today*, December 2014, accessed October 30, 2015, http://www.christianitytoday.com/amyjulia becker/2014/december/great-congruence-of-science-and-faith .html.

CONNECT WITH US!

CHARISMA HOUSE

(Spiritual Growth)

f Facebook.com/CharismaHouse

🐦 @CharismaHouse

📷 Instagram.com/CharismaHouseBooks

SILOAM

(Health)

📌 Pinterest.com/CharismaHouse

REALMS

(Fiction)

f Facebook.com/RealmsFiction